David Milne was born in The Wirral and educated at the University College of North Wales where he read modern languages and economics. He teaches at the University of Turin in Italy where he has lived for the last twenty years. However, it was his work as free-lance interpreter and translator that first took him to the Eastern Caribbean in 1984 and led him to take up travel writing. Since then he has visited the region on several occasions.

Dedication

To Elvi, for all her encouragement and patience.

Acknowledgements

The author wishes to extend his grateful thanks to all those who kindly assisted him with his research in Barbados. In particular he would like to thank the Barbados Board of Tourism (for photographs on pages 33, 58, 64, 65, 82, 94, 97, 107, 128) and the Barbados National Trust for all the support they offered. He also wishes to thank Ileana Gilardi for her kind assistance in preparing the maps used in this book.

Front cover: *Southern Palms — one of the top south coast hotels that offers plenty of water sports and evening entertainment.*

Lascelles Caribbean Guides

A Traveller's Guide

David Milne

Roger Lascelles, Cartographic and Travel Publisher

47 York Road, Brentford, Middlesex TW8 OQP. Tel: 081-847 0935

Publication Data

Title	Barbados
Typeface	Phototypeset in Compugraphic Times
Photographs	By the Author and the Barbados Board of Tourism
Index	Jane Thomas
Printing	Kelso Graphics, Kelso, Scotland.
ISBN	0 903909 93 6
Edition	First Jun 1991
Publisher	Roger Lascelles
	47 York Road, Brentford, Middlesex, TW8 0QP.
Copyright	David Milne

Distribution

Africa:	South Africa —	Faradawn, Box 17161, Hillbrow 2038
Americas:	Canada —	International Travel Maps & Books, P.O. Box 2290, Vancouver BC V6B 3W5
Asia:	India —	English Book Store, 17-L Connaught Circus/P.O. Box 328, New Delhi 110 001
	Singapore —	Graham Brash Pte Ltd., 36-C Prinsep St
Australasia:	Australia —	Rex Publications, 413 Pacific Highway, Artarmon NSW 2064. 428 3566
Europe:	Belgium —	Brussels - Peuples et Continents
	Germany —	Available through major booksellers with good foreign travel sections
	GB/Ireland —	Available through all booksellers with good foreign travel sections
	Italy —	Libreria dell'Automobile, Milano
	Netherlands —	Nilsson & Lamm BV, Weesp
	Denmark —	Copenhagen - Arnold Busck, G.E.C. Gad, Boghallen, G.E.C. Gad
	Finland —	Helsinki — Akateeminen Kirjakauppa
	Norway —	Oslo - Arne Gimnes/J.G. Tanum
	Sweden —	Stockholm/Esselte, Akademi Bokhandel, Fritzes, Hedengrens Gothenburg/Gumperts, Esselte Lund/Gleerupska
	Switzerland —	Basel/Bider: Berne/Atlas; Geneve/Artou; Lausanne/Artou: Zurich/Travel Bookshop

Contents

Part 1: Preparation and Plans

1 Introducing Barbados
When to go 11 — Official information 11 —
Currency 12 — Budgeting for your holiday 12 —
Health precautions 14 — What to wear 14

2 How to get there
By air 15 — By sea 17 — Travel documents 18 —
Customs 19

3 Where to stay
The Gold Coast 21 — South-west coast 22 — Other
areas 23 — Prices 23 — Selection of hotels and
guest houses 24 — Self-catering accommodation 27
— Private rooms 28 — House and villa rental 29

4 Getting around
The road network and driving conditions 31 — Car
hire 32 — Scooter and bicycle hire 33 — Taxis 33
— Buses 34 — Excursions 34

5 Practical information for visitors
Airlines 37 — Banks 37 — Books and newspapers
38 — Driving licence 38 — Electricity 38 —
Embassies 39 — Medical facilities 39 — Pests and
dangers 39 — Postal services 40 — Public holidays
41 — Radio and television 41 — Telephones 41 —
Tipping 41 — Tourist information 42 — Water
supply 42

6 Food, drink and dining out
Introduction to Barbadian food 43 — Tropical fruit 44 — Island drinks 47 — Restaurants 47 — Information for self-caterers 50

7 The sporting life
Water sports 51 — Cricket — 52 — Fishing 53 — Golf 53 — Hiking 54 — Horse-riding 54 — Horse races 54 — Tennis 54

8 Night life and entertainment
Dinner shows 55 — Calypso and steel bands 56 — Jazz 57 — Discos and pubs 57 — Cinema and theatre 57 — Festivals 57

9 Shopping and souvenirs
Facilities and hours of business 59 — Duty-free shopping 59 — Souvenirs 60

Part 2: Background to Barbados

10 About the island
The island's geography 61 — Climate 62 — Flora 63 — Fauna 63 — Communications 64 — The economy 65

11 Historical outline
Amerinidian Barbados 71 — The early settlers 73 — Sugar, slavery and the plantation system 77 — Emancipation 80 — The years of crises 81 — Post-war developments 83

12 The people
Population 85 — Religion 86 — Government and politics 87 — Education and social welfare 90 — Cultural tradition 92

Part 3: Touring the island

13 Bridgetown and St Michael
History 95 — What to see 96 — Places of interest near Bridgetown 102

14 The west coast
Bridgetown to Holetown 105 — Holetown 106 — On to Speightstown 108 — Speightstown 109

15 St Peter and St Lucy
'Island in the Sun' 111 — Monkeys galore 114 —A windmill and a Great House 115 — The rugged north-east 116 — Animal Flower Cave 116 — More coast and a distillery 117

16 The centre and the east
St Thomas 119 — St Joseph and St Andrew 124 — The east coast 127 — St George: north 129

17 The south
St George: south 131 — St John 135 — St Philip 139 — Christ Church 143

Appendices

A Bibliography 145

B Wind force: the Beaufort Scale 146

C Useful conversion tables 148

D Some Carribean Recipes 152

Index

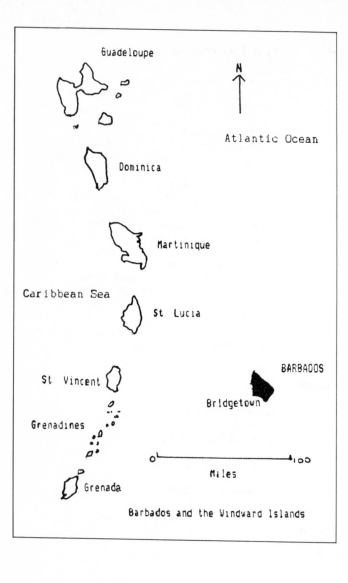

Guadeloupe

N

Atlantic Ocean

Dominica

Martinique

Caribbean Sea

St Lucia

St Vincent

BARBADOS

Bridgetown

Grenadines

0 _____ 100
Miles

Grenada

Barbados and the Windward Islands

ONE

Introducing Barbados

Twenty past eight on a hot August morning. The Moke stalls at a cross-roads in central Barbados. Tugging for all I can on the hand-brake to stop the vehicle rolling backwards, I try to start the engine again. Nothing doing. I curse my luck for we had booked in for the 9 o'clock visit to Harrison's Cave and we were still six or seven kilometres away. Stuck in the middle of nowhere, surrounded by sugar-cane fields and not a house in sight on this heavily populated island, let alone a public telephone. Two minutes later a car draws up behind us, the driver gets out and asks if he can help; his efforts at starting the Moke are no better than mine. We agree the only thing to do is to phone the car rental firm and ask them to send assistance. He invites us to hop in and whisks us off to a sugar factory to make our call and takes us back to the cross-roads where we now have the company of a broken down lorry. What had started as a frustrating experience turned out to be a short but fascinating talk on the woes of the Barbados sugar industry for our 'Good Samaritan' was a sugar farmer. A quarter of an hour later the mechanic arrives and fixes the Moke in a couple of minutes and we are back on the road. Our luck holds and when we reach Harrison's Cave at 9.15 we are told we have just missed the slide show but that we can board the train which is about to leave. Courtesy and kindness are things you most appreciate when you really need them, and the visitor to Barbados will discover that these are values that still count on this island, provided he or she is willing to reciprocate.

Glancing through the tour operators' brochures, I find the same clichés used to describe Barbados occurring time and time over: 'Little England', 'the most English of all West Indian islands', 'a long democratic tradition', 'England in the sun', 'a cricket-mad island', to be followed by an array of 'superb', 'super', 'marvellous', 'inviting', 'palm-fringed', 'great' beaches. Yes, the beaches are all you would expect them to be, beautiful, uncrowded

— just the place to relax and get a lovely tan. The hotels cater for all pockets ranging from modest self-catering accommodation to luxury class palaces where there are two members of staff for every guest and certainly you will experience no lack of evening entertainment. However, it would be wrong to judge an island only from its beaches and confine oneself to the self-contained luxury of the hotel complex. There are not the luxuriant rain forests of St Lucia or Dominica or the mountains of Jamaica, but the island does have two faces. Away from the built-up west and south coasts you will find rolling sugar-cane fields, striking cliffs and beautiful, breezy Atlantic coast lines and hundreds of kilometres of paved country lanes for you to explore. Over three hundred years of colonial history under British rule meant that there were no battles or revolutions here as part of the colonial power struggle — Barbados was the stronghold from where the British launched their attacks on other Caribbean islands, and as a consequence the island has much to offer of historical interest, including Jacobean Great Houses and fine parish churches. Most of its monuments have been restored, signposted and opened to visitors, but often the most satisfying experiences are those not advertised — getting off the beaten track, watching a game of beach cricket or dominoes, a visit to a remote pottery and stopping for a chat now and then.

Yet, on the other hand, we discover that Barbados is a forward-looking nation, with highly educated youth, a welfare state combined with a market economy, and all in all the island has managed its affairs extremely well since independence. It still considers itself a developing country but it is one of the more prosperous states in the West Indies, despite its shortage of raw materials. For better or worse tourism has made inroads into Barbadian society, most Bajans would agree it has improved their standard of living while realising the number of visitors cannot expand forever. Be that as it may the visitor — and Bajans prefer to consider you as such, rather than a tourist — is made to feel at home and helped to relax and get away from the stress of the outside world.

In this short book I have endeavoured to provide the reader not only with itineraries and information on where to stay, where to eat, what to do and how to do it, but also an island profile which I hope will give an insight into Barbadian life and institutions in the belief that an informed visitor will appreciate the subtle nuances of Barbados.

When to go

Its tropical location and the cooling trade winds ensure that Barbados offers holiday weather throughout the year. The difference in temperature between summer and winter is minimal (2° or 3° C). In general the winter months are also drier, with relative humidity as low as 57 per cent. However, the main reason why the winter months are the high season has little to do with local climatic differences but the phenomenon is mainly due to the fact that while you can bask in the sun in January in the Caribbean, North America and Europe can offer nothing better than snow, rain or fog. In the high season (16 December to 16 April) you will find that hotels are well booked up and the management tries to impose a certain formality and elegance, especially in the evenings. In the more exclusive resorts men will be expected to wear a jacket or tie for dinner. Besides the considerably higher hotel prices (in addition to which management sometimes imposes half-board conditions), obviously excursions and rental cars are in greater demand and require more advance booking. On the other hand, the high season guarantees the maximum choice of entertainment and you will never be lost for a dull moment. Low season bookings (the rest of the year) are becoming increasingly popular as visitors discover the advantages of lower prices (sometimes with a free week's accommodation), combined with better service and attractions such as Crop Over.

Official information

The Barbados Board of Tourism offers visitors and potential visitors up-to-date information on accommodation, island events and tourist attractions. Their courteous and experienced staff will be pleased to answer any queries you may have. The UK address is: Barbados Board of Tourism, 263 Tottenham Court Road, London W1P 9AA, tel. 071-636 9448/9; while the Head Office address is: Barbados Board of Tourism, P.O. Box 242, Harbour Road, Bridgetown, Barbados, W.1. tel. (809) 427-2623.

Consular enquiries should be addressed to: Barbados High Commission, 1 Great Russell Street, London WC1B 2NH, tel. 071-631 4975.

Currency

The official currency in Barbados is the Barbados dollar. This is pegged to the US dollar at the rate of US$1 = BDS$1.98. Naturally the exchange rate with other currencies reflects the strength or weakness of the US dollar. The visitor will find that the US dollar (both in banknotes and traveller's cheques) is widely accepted at hotels, restaurants and certain stores. Sterling notes and travellers' cheques are also accepted at hotels and of course at banks, where you will get a better exchange rate. There are no restrictions concerning the import or export of foreign currencies.

Barbados currency is available in banknotes of BDS$100, $50, $20, $10, $5, and coins of $1, 25c, 10c, 5c and 1c.

Credit cards such as Visa, Access/Mastercard and American Express are accepted by many establishments throughout the island. A credit card is particularly convenient when hiring a car as an open voucher can be left instead of a hefty deposit.

Budgeting for your holiday

The first problem in estimating the cost of visiting Barbados is the fluctuating exchange rate. Air fares are calculated in dollars and likewise hotel rates on Barbados, as the Barbadian dollar is pegged to the US dollar. Tour operators establish their catalogue prices months in advance and favourable fluctuations in the exchange rate are never passed on to the customer. 'In return' most operators try to keep surcharges and supplements to a minimum, offering various price guarantees. Read and consider all the options carefully before deciding about payment. The major cost of a Caribbean holiday is the air fare and this can indeed be offputting to anyone contemplating independent travel. The cheapest scheduled return flight (with early booking restrictions) is about £450 (to which you should add about £100 if you are planning travelling in July or August). Hotel prices could vary from about US$30 for a double room in summer in a modest guest house to US$250 and more in one of the top resorts. Winter rates are often 50-100 per cent higher. Obviously independent travelling has its advantages, costs not being one of them; no tour operator offers a night in charming Atlantic coast inns, for example, and being independent means you can really sample what the island has to offer. On the other hand, in such a small island 'returning to base' every day is no great problem as the furthest corner of the island is no more than an hour's drive away.

The cost of meals on Barbados is generally higher than in the UK and many tour operators advise clients to take the half-board option to avoid too many surprises. Certainly in this way it is easier to budget your holiday, but it does have its disadvantages in that it discourages you from visiting some of the island's more characteristic restaurants. Some hotels have attempted to offset this by offering a certain amount of flexibility with a scheme whereby the hotel allows its guests the possibility of dining in sister hotels on the island. Normally this type of arrangement is mentioned in travel brochures. A popular solution for keeping costs down is self-catering in one of Barbados's numerous apartels — this ensures flexibility at reasonable prices.

Rockley Resort — offers good moderately priced self catering accommodation and a 9-hole golf course. It is located just south of Bridgetown.

Health precautions

At the time of writing the Barbadian authorities do not require any Health Certificates from European or North American visitors unless they have previously visited countries where there is a risk of yellow fever. UK Health Authorities, however, do recommend vaccination against polio and typhoid and it is advisable to check arrangements with your family doctor in good time before your departure date. It should be remembered, on the other hand, that Barbados has one of the most salubrious climates in the West Indies, that sanitation conditions are generally good and that the island has an abundant supply of pure drinking water.

If you are on prescription medicine it is advisable to ask your doctor to prescribe an adequate amount for you to take with you. Pharmacies on the island are well stocked with North American and British specialities so there is no need to take enormous first aid kits with you. Insect repellents and insecticides are readily available locally. If you are unfortunate and become ill or have an accident you will find a good medical service and well qualified doctors and dentists. You should remember that there is no reciprocal health agreement between the UK and Barbados and therefore it is essential to have adequate medical insurance.

Sunburn can easily ruin your holiday and the cooling trade wind breezes can be very deceiving. Use high protection-factor screens and above all take the tanning very easy, especially in the first few days.

What to wear

Obviously in a tropical climate lightweight natural fibre clothes are the order of the day. The general tone is casual and informal but you will find that during the high season the smarter hotels and restaurants expect men to wear a jacket and tie. If you are doing business a jacket is not necessary, since normal business dress for men is a long-sleeved shirt and a tie.

As in most of ex-British West Indies you will find that people tend to dress up when they go into town, and beachwear and mini-shorts are definitely not acceptable anywhere except on the beaches or around the pool.

TWO

How to get there

By air

Barbados has one of the finest airports in the West Indies with an 11,000-foot runway that can easily handle the biggest of planes, including Concorde. Today Grantley Adams International Airport not only handles traffic destined for the island itself but is a hub for regional traffic, with good connections to North and South America and the rest of the Caribbean, both on scheduled and charter planes. Travelling time from Britain is about eight hours, normally with daylight flights on the outward journey and night flights on the homeward leg.

Scheduled flights

Two airlines offer regular connections with Barbados from Britain: British Airways and BWIA International.

British Airways has several flights a week from London (Heathrow and Gatwick) using B747s. Some of the flights are direct whilst others fly via Antigua. To facilitate passengers from the north of England some of the Gatwick flights pick up passengers at Manchester.

BWIA International is the flag carrier of Trinidad and Tobago, but for almost fifty years has also been the de facto carrier for the south Caribbean. At the time of writing, it provides two non-stop flights a week from Heathrow on its Tristar wide-bodied aircraft.

Demand for Caribbean flights is heavy, especially in December/January and July/August and early bookings are advisable. An important point to bear in mind is that even if you have booked a return flight this must be reconfirmed once you have arrived in the Caribbean. Prices vary according to the type of ticket and the season — ironically while winter is the high season for hotels in Barbados it is the low season for flights.

Charter flights

Several UK tour operators are now offering 'all inclusive' packages using charter flights from Stansted, Luton and Manchester. Only a few years ago this type of holiday was not encouraged on Barbados which was looking upmarket. The question is still a matter of some controversy, but it has been recognised that low price holidays do solve the problems of many of the medium- and lower-priced hotels, especially during the low season. A two-week package deal offered by one of the big charter operators is likely to cost you about £100 less than a package in the same hotel, but using scheduled airlines. On the other hand, it should be borne in mind that particularly in busy holiday periods airport delays for charter passengers tend to be long and seating is more cramped, an important factor on a long flight. If you pay a supplement you are entitled to more spacious seating but at that point it may be better to choose a scheduled flight.

'Seat only' tickets do not seem to be available on charter flights to Barbados, but you could try looking at the advertisements in Sunday newspapers.

On arrival

You will be issued with an immigration card during your flight. This should be completed and handed over to the immigration officer at the airport, together with your passport and your return or onward ticket. You will be handed back a copy of the immigration card which you should keep carefully as this must be handed in on departure. Immigration control at Grantley Adams International airport is fairly straightforward but rather slow. If you are travelling on a jumbo you should count on at least 45 minutes to pass through immigration and customs. The immigration officer will want to know where you will be staying in Barbados and if you have not booked accommodation you should seek assistance from the Tourist Board as you enter the hall.

The modern terminal has all the usual facilities including a bureau de change, a Tourist Board office, duty-free shops, a restaurant, snack bars and car-hire firms. The bureau de change is open from 8.00 am to midnight and is conveniently situated just after immigration control but before customs. It can also be used by departing passengers after they have gone through passport control and customs. When you pick up your luggage you will find eager porters or 'red caps' ready to whisk it away to the taxi rank. The present charge is BDS$0.75 per piece. In any case the distance to the taxi rank is short. If you are travelling with a tour company the representatives meet incoming passengers in the hall after immigration and then arrange taxis or mini-buses to the hotels. If you are travelling individually you will find no shortage of taxis — remember to check the fare before you get in. You will find a list of indicative fares in the chapter 'Getting around'. There is no regular airport bus but you will find a public bus service into Bridgetown — the bus stop is located on the main road, a short distance from the airport. Travelling with luggage on buses is inadvisable as they are often very crowded.

Departure by air

The first thing to remember is to reconfirm your return booking in good time. If you do not do this you may find you have no seat. If you are travelling with a tour operator your representative will normally make the necessary arrangements. At the time of writing if you are travelling British Airways you cannot obtain a seat number in advance, so if you want to try to get a particular seat make sure you arrive in good time. For intercontinental flights it is advisable to arrive at the airport at least two hours before departure time. All passengers must pay a departure tax of BDS$20 when they check in and they will also be asked for their copy of the immigration card. If you wish to use the airport restaurant remember you must do so before you pass through immigration control, otherwise you will have to make do with bar snacks. After going through passport control and customs you will enter the departure lounge where you will find a variety of shops, including duty-free stores. You will also find the pick-up point for certain duty-free goods (such as spirits and cigarettes) that you may have purchased in town.

By sea

Banana boats

For individual travellers who do not have a problem of time or who do not like flying, there is an alternative way of reaching the island — by banana boat. Geest Lines (P.O. Box 20, Barry, Glamorgan CF6 8XE) offer weekly sailings from South Wales to Barbados and the Windward Islands. In this way the traveller can visit several West Indian islands, maybe stopping off for a week and catching the next boat. Demand for the comfortable but limited passenger accommodation is heavy and ample advance booking is essential.

Cruise ships
Cruising in the Caribbean too offers the chance to visit Barbados. Many cruise lines feature a stop in Barbados but to enjoy the island fully you should choose a line that offers the possibility of combining a cruise with a stay on the island. The Cunard Line, for example, has its own hotel on Barbados and is pleased to arrange this combination. Your travel agent will be able to advise you on the latest cruise and fly-and-cruise programmes.

Arrival and departure by ship
Cruise ship passengers will arrive at Bridgetown Harbour. This deep water facility was completed in 1961 and can accommodate several cruise ships at the same time. The harbour is located about a kilometre (half a mile) north of the city, to which it is connected by the Princess Alice Highway. Passengers will find few formalities at the harbour other than routine passport control. Cruise ships usually arrive in the early morning and depart in the evening. Excursions can usually be booked on board ship. If you wish to do your own touring you will find plenty of taxis at the harbour. There is also a Tourist Board booth and a bureau de change. Last minute shoppers may be interested in the handicraft stalls conveniently located at Pelican Village, just outside the harbour zone, while those who have made duty-free purchases in town will be able to pick them up at customs.

Travel documents

UK citizens require a valid full passport or a British Visitor's passport for entry into Barbados. The British Visitor's passport is valid for bona fide tourists who intend to stay less than 90 days on the island. No visa is required.

Other EC citizens require a valid passport for entry. US and Canadian citizens require only proof of citizenship (such as birth certificate or passport) and may stay for up to six months. Other nationalities should enquire at the Barbados High Commission (London office: 1 Great Russell Street, London WC1B 3NH, tel: 071-631 4975) or at the nearest Barbados Embassy.

All visitors must provide the immigration officer with their address on the island and possess a return or onward ticket. Visitors have to complete an immigration card (distributed during the flight) and keep the carbon copy.

If you intend to drive a motor vehicle during your stay on the island, don't forget to take your driving licence which must be produced to obtain a local registration certificate. An international driving licence is not necessary.

Customs

Visitors may be subject to import duties except for personal effects, including cameras and sports equipment. You are also allowed 735 grammes (26 oz) of spirits, 0.23 kilos (½lb) of tobacco and 50 cigars or one carton of cigarettes. If you plan to import conference material or gifts you should get clearance from Customs. You may not import pets without having obtained a permit in advance from the Ministry of Agriculture, Graeme Hall, Christ Church.

Villa Nova Great House (St John). A fine early nineteenth century property that was once the home of Lord Avon.

THREE

Where to stay

Barbados offers one of the best ranges of accommodation in the Caribbean with over 150 establishments providing around 14,500 beds. Furthermore the long tradition of hospitality on the island and the early start of its hotel industry have meant that it can provide a high standard of courteous and thoughtful service. Accommodation may vary from self-catering studios to luxury 300-room properties, from small family-run guest houses to villa rental. What you will not find, fortunately, are high-rise buildings — hotels usually blend into tropical gardens. Naturally most establishments are located on or near the beach, and even a short walk can bring prices tumbling. The two main development concentrations are in the parishes of St James on the west coast and Christ Church in the south west.

The Gold Coast

The parish of St James is sometimes known as the 'Gold Coast' or the 'Platinum Coast' and as such names suggest it is definitely upmarket, with the idyllic calm leeward waters of the Caribbean, beautiful sandy beaches lined with palms and casuarinas and some of the Caribbean's top resorts such as Sandy Lane, Colony Club, Glitter Bay, Royal Pavilion, just to name a few . Luxury and excellence of service here are a byword. In recent years west coast development has extended northwards into the parish of St Peter — the construction of Heywoods Resort, for example, has led to the revamping of the northern town of Speightstown and is encouraging entrepreneurs to set up other facilities. As mentioned before, the west coast is mainly upmarket, but there are pleasant exceptions for those looking for simpler accommodation at reasonable prices. Self-catering facilities exist at Sunset Crest, Holetown, while the Sandridge Hotel in St Peter is extremely popular with British guests and can offer a range of traditional hotel and self-catering services. For those who wish a wonderful 'get away from it all' holiday the Sugar Cane Club, perched on a hill in St Peter (15 minutes' walk from the sea) offers good value for money and a unique opportunity to see monkeys in their natural surroundings.

South-west coast

Development in Christ Church, on the other hand, stretches from Hastings, just south of Bridgetown, through Rockley, Worthing, St Lawrence to Maxwell, near Oistins. Here the industry has followed another pattern, generally smaller properties (although there are notable exceptions) offering good value for money and the south coast has earned the reputation of being lively, rather than sedate and exclusive. Christ Church is in fact a highly populated parish with much suburban housing, interspersed with excellent shopping facilities as well as a myriad of restaurants, hotels, apartels and holiday flats. The sea is still the Caribbean but this coast is a little breezier, making excellent conditions for windsurfers, and surprisingly the beaches are never crowded. The greatest tourist concentration is at St Lawrence Gap, a sort of bulge on the coast that allows a secondary road to form a crescent on the seaward side of Highway 7. Two large properties Southwinds and Southern Palms, set in fine gardens offer a wide choice of accommodation, restaurants and especially entertainment in the evening and, as a result, they act as magnets for guests staying in smaller establishments. The Casuarina Beach Club set at the quiet end of the bulge is a popular choice for those who wish seclusion but at the same time to be within walking distance of other hotels. Most of the development in Hastings and Rockley is along Highway 7 and you may have the problem of the noise of traffic in certain rooms, although the situation has eased since the West Coast-Airport Highway was opened. Very pleasant hotel and self-catering accommodation can be found in the attractive 'clusters' of the Rockley Resort which is located off the main road and boasts its own 9-hole golf course.

Other areas

Other areas with hotels include Aquatic Gap near Bridgetown where the Hilton and Grand Barbados Beach Resort provide accommodation for holiday-makers and business-persons alike, and St Philip, where there are a few exclusive properties such as Sam Lord's Castle and the Crane. (Remember that the sea can be rough on the south-east coast and swimming dangerous.) The extremely beautiful Atlantic coast offers little in the way of accommodation as the area has still managed to preserve its unspoilt nature. Those tempted to spend some time here could choose the charming colonial atmosphere of the Kingsley Club at Cattlewash (St Joseph) and find a type of holiday that appeals to old Barbadian families.

Prices

There is no official classification of hotel accommodation as yet, although this has been in the offing for several years. However, the Barbados Board of Tourism does issue two price lists per year (winter rates cover the period 16 December to 15 April while the

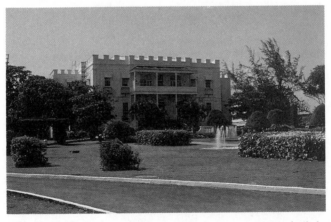

Sam Lord's Castle (St Philip). A lavish Regency mansion built by a man who had a reputation as a pirate. According to legend he attracted ships to the rocks below the castle by hanging lanterns from the trees. Today the castle is part of a luxurious hotel complex.

summer list is for the rest of the year). Prices are in US dollars and are not inclusive of a 5 per cent Government tax. Most establishments add a further 10 per cent service charge. As mentioned in the previous chapter prices fluctuate considerably between the two seasons and in many cases you can expect to pay 50-100 per cent more in winter. Some hotels also offer free weeks in the summer (but sometimes attach conditions such as compulsory half board).

The list which follows (based on Tourist Board publications) indicates price ranges as follows:

L = Luxury   M = Medium price range
U = Upper price range   Mo = Moderate price range

It also indicates the number of rooms, followed by a series of numbers to indicate the facilities available.

1 Full board available   9 On the beach
2 Half board available   10 Commissary on premises
3 B&B terms available   11 Suites available
4 Room only rates available   12 Some rooms with kitchenettes
5 Children's rates available 13 Swimming pool
6 10% service charge   14 Tennis courts
7 Air conditioning available 15 Golf course
8 Air conditioning inclusive 16 Squash

Selection of hotels and guest houses

West coast — St James and St Peter
Barbados Beach Village Fitts Bay, St James, tel. 425-1440. (Price range M; rooms 88 - 2, 5, 6, 7, 8, 9, 10, 11, 13, 14)
Bella Beach Tropicana Lower Carlton, St James , tel. 422-2277 (Price range Mo; rooms 24 - 2, 5, 6, 7, 8, 9, 11, 12)
Buccaneer Bay Paynes Bay, St James, tel. 432-7981. (Price range U; rooms 30 - 2, 5, 6, 7, 8, 9, 10, 11, 12, 13)
Chrizel's Garden Gibbs, St Peter, tel. 422-2403. (Price range Mo/M; rooms 7 - 1, 2, 3, 5, 6, 10, 11, 12)
Cobber's Cove Road View, St Peter, tel. 422-2291 (Price range L; rooms 38 - 5, 6, 7, 8, 9, 10, 11, 12, 13)
Coconut Creek Derricks, St James, tel. 432-0803 (Price range U; rooms 52 - 5, 6, 7, 8, 9, 13)
Colony Club Porters, St James, tel. 422-2335 (Price range U; rooms 75 - 5, 6, 7, 8, 9, 10, 13)

Coral Reef St James, tel. 422-2372 (Price range U/L; rooms 75 - 5, 6, 7, 8, 9, 13, 14)

Discovery Bay Holetown, St James, tel. 432-1301 (Price range U; rooms 84 - 2, 5, 6, 7, 8, 9, 10, 11, 14)

Divi St James Vauxhall, St James, tel. 432-7840 (Price range U; rooms 131 - 1, 2, 3, 6, 7, 8, 9, 10, 11, 13, 16)

Glitter Bay Porters, St James, tel. 422-4111 (Price range U/L; rooms 86 - 2, 5, 6, 7, 8, 9, 10, 11, 12, 13, 14)

Heywoods St Peter, tel. 422-2275 (Price range M/U; rooms 306 - 2, 5, 6, 7, 8, 9, 10, 11, 12, 13, 14, 15, 16)

Inn On The Beach Holetown, St James, tel. 432-0385 (Price range M; rooms 21 - 2, 5, 6, 8, 9, 10, 13, 14)

King's Beach Hotel Mullins, St Peter, tel. 422-1690 (Price range M/U; rooms 57 - 2, 5, 6, 8, 9, 10, 13, 14)

Royal Pavilion Porters, St James, tel. 422-4444 (Price range L; rooms 75 - 2, 5, 6, 7, 8, 9, 10, 11, 13, 14)

Sandpiper Inn St James, tel. 422-2251 (Price range U/L; rooms 46 - 4, 5, 6, 7, 8, 9, 10, 13, 14)

Sandridge Road View, St Peter, tel. 422-2361 (Price range M; rooms 52 - 2, 5, 6, 7, 8, 9, 11, 12, 13)

Sandy Lane St James, tel. 432-1311 (Price range L; rooms 112 - 5, 6, 7, 8, 9, 10, 11, 12, 14, 15)

Settler's Beach St James, tel. 422-3052 (Price range U; rooms 22 - 2, 5, 6, 7, 8, 9, 11, 12, 13)

Smuggler's Cove Paynes Bay, St James, tel. 432-1741 (Price range M; rooms 21 - 2, 5, 6, 7, 8, 9, 12, 13)

Sugar Cane Club Maynards, St Peter, tel. 422-5026 (Price range Mo; rooms 20 - 2, 5, 7, 11, 13)

Tamarind Cove Paynes Bay, St James, tel. 432-1332 (Price range U; rooms 88 - 5, 6, 7, 8, 9, 13)

Treasure Beach Paynes Bay, St James, tel. 432-1346 (Price range U; rooms 25 - 2, 5, 6, 7, 8, 9, 11, 12, 13)

St Michael (near Bridgetown)

Cunard Paradise Black Rock, St Michael, tel. 424-0888 (Price range U; rooms 172 - 2, 5, 6, 7, 8, 9, 10, 13, 14)

Grand Barbados Beach Resort St Michael, tel. 426-0890 (Price range U/L; rooms 133 - 1, 2, 3, 5, 6, 7, 8, 9, 10, 11, 13)

Hilton International Needhams Point, St Michael, tel. 426-0200 (Price range M/L; rooms 185 - 2, 5, 6, 7, 8, 9, 10, 11, 13, 14)

Fortitude Guest House Wellington Street, Bridgetown, tel. 426-4210 (Price range Mo; rooms 6 - 5)

South-west coast — Christ Church

Abbeville Rockley, Christ Church. (Price range Mo; rooms 21 - 5, 7, 8, 13)

Accra Rockley, Christ Church, tel. 427-7866 (Price range M; rooms 52 - 2, 5, 6, 7, 8, 9, 11, 12, 13)

Andrea on Sea St Lawrence Gap, Christ Church, tel. 428-6021 (Price range Mo; rooms 76 - 2, 5, 6, 7, 8, 10, 11, 13)

Asta Hastings, Christ Church, tel. 427-2541 (Price range M; rooms 60 - 2, 3, 5, 7, 8, 9, 10, 11, 12, 13)

Barbados Windsurfing Club Maxwell, Christ Church, tel.428-9095 (Price range M; rooms 15 - 5, 6, 9, 10, 12)

Best Western Sandy Beach Worthing, Christ Church, tel. 428-9033 (Price range U; rooms 89 - 2, 5, 6, 7,8, 9, 11, 12, 13)

Blue Horizon Rockley, Christ Church, tel. 427-7246 (Price range M; rooms 118 - 5, 7, 10, 12, 13)

Bresmay St Lawrence Gap, Christ Church, tel. 428-6131 (Price range M; rooms 50 - 5, 6, 7, 8, 9, 10, 11, 12, 13)

Caribee Hastings, Christ Church, tel. 436-6232 (Price range M; rooms 55 - 2, 5, 6, 7, 8, 9, 12)

Casuarina Dover, Christ Church, tel.428-3600 (Price range M/U; rooms 100 - 2, 5, 6, 7, 8, 9, 11, 12, 13, 14, 16)

Coconut Court Hastings, Christ Church, tel. 427-1655 (Price range M; rooms 61 - 5, 9, 11, 12, 13)

Dover Beach St Lawrence, Christ Church, tel. 428-7181 (Price range M; rooms 27 - 2, 5, 6, 7, 8, 9, 12, 13, 14)

Fairholme Maxwell, Christ Church, tel. 428-9425 (Price range Mo; rooms 31 - 2, 5, 6, 7, 8, 12, 13)

Golden Beach Hastings, Christ Church, tel. 429-5818 (Price range Mo/M; rooms 25 - 2, 5, 6, 7, 8, 9, 12, 13)

Half Moon St Lawrence Gap, Christ Church, tel. 428-7131 (Price range M; rooms 29 - 2, 5, 6, 7, 8, 9, 11, 13)

Ocean View Hastings, Christ Church, tel. 427-7821 (Price range M; rooms 35 - 2, 5, 6, 7, 8, 9, 11)

Rainbow Reef Dover, Christ Church, tel. 428-5110 (Price range Mo/M; rooms 43 - 2, 5, 6, 7, 8, 9, 11, 12, 13)

Regency Cove Hastings, Christ Church, tel. 427-7924 (Price range Mo/M; rooms 30 - 2, 5, 6, 7, 8, 11, 12, 13)

Rockley Resort Golf Club Road, Christ Church, tel. 435-7880 (Price range M; rooms 111 - 2, 5, 7, 8, 10, 11, 12, 13, 14, 15, 16)

San Remo Maxwell, Christ Church, tel. 428-2822 (Price range Mo; rooms 23 - 2, 5, 7, 9, 12)

Sand Acres Maxwell, Christ Church, tel. 428-7141 (Price range M; rooms 37 - 2, 5, 7, 8, 9, 11, 12, 13, 14)

Sichris Worthing, Christ Church, tel. 435-7930 (Price range M; rooms 24 - 2, 5, 6, 7, 8, 11, 12, 13)

Silver Sands Silver Sands, Christ Church, tel. 428-6001 (Price range M; rooms 106 - 2, 3, 5, 6, 7, 8, 9, 10, 11, 12, 13, 14)

Southern Palms St Lawrence Gap, Christ Church, tel. 428-7171 (Price range M/U; rooms 93 - 2, 5, 6, 7, 8, 9, 10, 11, 12, 13, 14)

Southwinds St Lawrence Gap, Christ Church, tel. 428-7308 (Price range U; rooms 160 - 2, 5, 6, 7, 8, 9, 10, 11, 12, 13, 14)

Spinnakers St Lawrence Gap, Christ Church, tel. 428-7308 (Price range Mo; rooms 9 - 2, 5, 7, 8, 9, 11, 12)

Sunhaven Rockley, Christ Church, tel. 427-3550 (Price range M; rooms 35 - 2, 5, 7, 8, 9, 10, 11, 13)

Welcome Inn Maxwell, Christ Church, tel. 428-9900 (Price range M; rooms 110 - 2, 5, 6, 7, 8, 9, 10, 11, 12, 13)

Worthing Court Worthing, Christ Church, tel. 435-7910 (Price range Mo/M; rooms 24 - 2, 5, 6, 7, 8, 11, 12, 13)

South-east coast - St Philip

Crane Crane Beach, St Philip, tel. 423-6220 (Price range U; rooms 25 - 2, 5, 6, 9, 10, 11, 13, 14)

Ginger Bay St Philip, tel. 423-5810 (Price range U; rooms 16 - 2, 4, 5, 6, 9, 11, 13, 14)

Marriott's Sam Lord's Castle St Philip, tel. 423-7350 (Price range U; rooms 256 - 2, 5, 6, 7, 8, 9, 10, 11, 13, 14)

Robin's Nest Long Bay, St Philip, tel. 423-6088 (Price range Mo; rooms 17 - 2, 5, 7, 8, 12, 13)

East coast - St Joseph

Kingsley Club Cattlewash, St Joseph, tel. 433-9422 (Price range Mo; rooms 7 - 2, 5, 6)

Atlantis Hotel Bathsheba, St Joseph, tel. 433-9445 (Price range Mo; rooms 14 - 2,5,6,9)

Self-catering accommodation

This list indicates the number of units, followed by key numbers to indicate the features available.

1 3 - bedroom accom. available
2 4 - bedroom accom. available
3 Maid service
4 Air conditioning available
5 Air conditioning inclusive
6 Swimming pool
7 Tennis courts
8 On the beach
9 Commissary on premises
10 Limited dining facilities

West coast

Caribbean House Paynes Bay, St James, tel. 432-1375 (Units 31 - 3, 4, 5, 6, 9, 10)

Golden Palm Beach Apartments Sunset Crest, St James, tel. 432-6666 (Units 71 - 3, 4, 6, 8)

Homar Rentals Sunset Crest, St James, tel. 432-6750 (Units 104 - 3, 4, 6, 7, 9)

Na-Diesie Holetown, St James, tel. 432-0469 (Units 20 - 3, 4, 5, 8)

New Haven Mansion Gibbs, St Peter, tel. 422-2537 (Units 6 - 1, 2, 3, 4, 6)

Palm Beach Holetown, St James, tel. 432-1384 (Units 30 - 3, 4, 6, 8, 10)

Sun Rentals Sunset Crest, St James, tel. 427-1234 (Units 65 - 3, 4, 6, 7, 10)

South-west coast

Blythwood — Worthing, Christ Church, tel. 435-7712 Units 14 - 3, 4, 5, 6, 8)

Fedey Dover, Christ Church, tel. 428-4051 (Units 12 - 3, 4, 5, 10)

Magic Isle Rockley, Christ Church, tel. 427-7382 (Units 30 - 3, 4, 5, 6, 8)

Maresol St Lawrence Gap, Christ Church, tel. 428-9300 (Units 12 - 3, 4, 8, 9)

Rockley Resort Golf Club Road, Christ Church, tel. 435-7880 (1, 2, 3, 4, 5, 6, 9, 11)

Rostrevor St Lawrence Gap, Christ Church, tel. 428-9298 (Units 44 - 1, 3, 6, 8, 9, 10)

Shangri La Maxwell, Christ Church (Units 43 - 3, 4, 5, 6, 9)

St Lawrence St Lawrence Gap, Christ Church, tel. 422-4444 (Units 75 - 3, 4, 5, 6, 8, 9)

Woodville Worthing, Christ Church, tel. 427-1498 (Units 28 - 3, 4, 5, 6, 8)

East coast

Fleet View Apartments Bathsheba, St Joseph, tel. 433-9422

Private rooms

There is also a limited number of landlords who are willing to rent out accommodation in private houses to visitors. Those interested in comfortable but economic rooms in the Bridgetown area, for example, may contact: Ms C. Phillips, 'Silverton', Aquatic Gap (near Brown Sugar restaurant), St Michael, tel. 427-3265

House and villa rental

For those interested in property rental the island has a good selection of houses and villas for short, medium or long leases, or indeed for purchase if you are interested in a long-term solution. Maids, cooks, gardeners and other staff are readily available. For further information on this subject, contact: Fairways Real Estate, Rockley Resort, Christ Church.

View over the wild and rugged east coast.

Morgan Lewis Windmill (St Andrew). This National Trust property allows us to imagine the Barbadian landscape of the 18th century when hundreds of such mills dotted the countryside. The mills were used for crushing sugar-cane and were driven by the constant trade winds which cool the island.

FOUR

Getting around

The road network and driving conditions

Barbados offers over 1200 kilometres (800 miles) of paved road, which on such a small island is an awful lot. The main roads are known as 'Highways' and radiate out from Bridgetown, being numbered from 1 to 7. You will also find that when Highways branch then a letter is added, for example, Highway 3B. The other roads seem to have no classification. Recently a new Highway has been built from the airport to just north of Bridgetown. This also has the function of a ring road round the city and has eased congestion considerably as it links up all the other Highways. Work is under way on the extension of this road northwards to Speightstown. You will find 'free' maps available at hotels or at the Tourist Board offices. If you wish to buy a more accurate map (but some of the tourist spots are not marked on it), you will find an Ordnance Survey map, complete with an index compiled by the National Trust, in the leading book stores.

Road conditions vary very much from the new smooth highways to bumpy country lanes. Barbados has gone metric so distances and speed limits are in kilometres or kilometres per hour. The general speed limit is 60 kph out of town (raised to 80 kph on Spring Garden Highway) and 32 kph in built-up areas. Most drivers will find the limits are fairly realistic bearing in mind road conditions. Roads in and around the capital tend to be very busy but quiet in rural areas. Driving is British-style on the left. Parking can be tricky in Bridgetown as there are now quite a few 'No Parking' zones, where parking will probably cost you a fine in the Magistrate's Court. The island has a good network of petrol stations, especially on the west and south coasts.

Note that if you wish to drive in Barbados you must first obtain a temporary permit (registration certificate) by presenting your national or international licence to the car rental company or at certain police stations. The cost of the operation is currently BDS$10 and the certificate is valid for 12 months.

Car hire

Car rental is very popular in Barbados and you will find a large number of firms offering anything from the ubiquitous Moke to Japanese saloon cars. In most cases the car is delivered to your hotel and the registration certificate is issued on the spot. Normally there is a supplement for collison waiver insurance — if you do not wish to accept this then you will be responsible for the first BDS$500 of a claim (or more if the driver is under 22). Hire costs vary from firm to firm but the average weekly charge for a Moke or a small saloon is BDS$400-450 (unlimited mileage). Daily rates start from about BDS$90. The condition of the cars, especially the Mokes, can vary enormously and generally speaking you should not expect to find a vehicle in 'mint' condition. Advance booking is recommended in the high season and at Crop Over (late July/early August) when demand outstrips supply.

Some of the more reputable firms are:

Avis tel. 428-7202 (airport); 425-1388 (Bridgetown)
Budget tel. 427-5094 (St Michael)
Courtesy tel. 426-5871 (St Michael)
Dear's tel. 429-9277 (Bridgetown)
Drive-A-Matic tel. 422-2361 (Speightstown)
Hertz tel. 428-7878 (airport); 427-5094 (Bridgetown)
Sunny Isle Motors tel. 428-2965
Sunset Crest Rent-A-Car tel. 432-1482 (Holetown)

Opposite: *(Courtesy of Jolly Roger Cruises) One of two Jolly Roger pirate ships that ply the placid west coast offering a fun-filled trip, music, food and unlimited drinks.*

Scooter and bicycle hire

Scooters and mopeds can be hired from Jumbo Vehicle Rentals, Dayrells Road, St Michael (tel. 426-5689). Rates vary from about BDS$145 to 275 a week. Helmets and insurance included.
Bicycle hire Mountain bikes are available for hire from M.A. Williams, Hastings, Christ Church (tel. 427-1043). Delivery and collection can be arranged.

Taxis

There are over 1,000 taxis (which can be recognised by the 'Z' number plate) in service on the island and Barbadian taxi drivers are generally well informed on the island's tourist attractions. However, if you are planning to hire a taxi for the day it is better to go with a driver who has been recommended to you by the hotel or friends. Taxis can be found at ranks in the city and outside many hotels.

Although the cabs are not metered there is a Government list of standard fares, but in any case you are advised to check the fare with the driver before getting in and make sure that he is quoting in Barbados dollars and not US dollars (worth about double). Here are some examples of the fares (in BDS$) from the official list:

from the airport to:		*from Central Bridgetown to:*	
Speightstown	42	Harbour	6
Heywoods	42	Bathsheba	38
Bathsheba	36	Speightstown	27
Holetown	30	Holetown	20
Central Bridgetown	23	Harrison's Cave	24
South coast	16	St Lawrence	13

Hourly rates should not exceed $31 for the first hour and $21 for each additional hour. Waiting time: day $7; night $8.

Opposite: *The coral reef off Barbados' west coast offers good opportunities for scuba fans.*

Buses

Barbados boasts one of the best bus services in the Caribbean, with the blue and yellow trim Transport Board buses plying the highways and byways. Most bus routes lead to Bridgetown but some are based on Speightstown and Oistins. The bus stops are marked 'to city' and 'out of city'; you should signal the driver to stop. There is no official timetable but buses on the main routes are fairly frequent and run until late in the evening. There is a flat fare of BDS$1 and you should have the exact fare to pop in the fare box. There is a conductor whose duty seems to be confined to handing out the tickets. Tokens can be purchased at bus stations and there is a small discount if you buy 10. The buses are often crowded, especially in the rush hour (which is from 4 to 6 in the afternoon), and you can expect an 'exhilarating' ride. Buses for the south of the island are based on the modern bus station in Fairchild Street, while those for the west coast and the north leave from Lower Green. Speightstown too boasts a fine modern bus station with services mainly to Bridgetown, the north and east.

There is also a private mini-bus service running on the more popular (and profitable) routes. The mini-buses are only slightly smaller than the Transport Board buses but their livery is yellow with blue trim and they can be recognised by their blaring music. Usually the mini-buses have a quicker turn-around time and are very popular with young people. The fare is the same as that of Transport Board buses. In Bridgetown they are based at Temple Yard (for north and west coast destinations) and Probyn Square (for the south).

Excursions

Tourism is big business on this island and you will find that Barbados offers a host of well organised excursions to lighten the visitor's pocket. Below you will find a summary of the most popular excursions which can be booked through your tour representative, your hotel or directly through the company organising the tour.

Island coach tours
These are particularly popular with visitors who do not intend to hire a car and visit the island themselves. Both full-day and half-day tours are available. The full-day tour will include a visit to many of the island's beauty spots, including the north and east coasts with

lunch provided, while the half-day tour is normally to Harrison's Cave and the Flower Forest. The largest operator in this field is L.E. Williams Tour Co. Ltd. (tel. 427-1043) with pick ups directly from your hotel.

Coastal cruises

Coastal cruising in Barbados has a character all of its own — you will find everything from exclusive yachts to private parties or paddle steamers, depending on your mood.

The Jolly Roger organisation (tel. 436-6424) has two twin 'pirate' sailing vessels that offer four-hour daytime and sunset cruises from Bridgetown harbour. The ships sail up the west coast to near Holetown where the crew provide a barbecue lunch or dinner. The accent is on having a good time with the crew providing entertainment and offering passengers the chance to try 'walking the plank' or rope-swinging. There is plenty of music too, which accompanied by an unlimited supply of free rum punch ensures that everybody has a good time.

The alternative fun-boat is the 'Bajan Queen', a Mississippi-style cruise boat based in Bridgetown harbour and offering daytime and evening cruises. Nice buffet and open bar. Plenty of music for dancing. For reservations call 436-2149.

If you fancy a different sort of cruise, the excitement of sailing with a small party on a big catamaran and maybe a bit of snorkelling thrown in, then you might well be interested in the 'Irish Mist II' which leaves from the Careenage. It offers lunchtime and afternoon sailings. For further information phone 436-9201.

An alternative to catamaran sailing could be yachting on one of the several luxury yachts that ply for hire. Generally all offer standard four-hour cruises with lunch and open bar as well as snorkelling facilities. Good examples of such craft are 'Carib Girl' and 'Secret Love' (for the latter phone 432-1972).

Atlantis submarine

While being one of the more expensive excursions (US$58 at time of writing) — and understandably so for the cost of the organisation and equipment — a dive down to the coral reef is one of the highlights of many a Barbadian holiday. The party of up to 24 passengers assembles at the company's office at the Careenage before being whisked out to sea on a comfortable launch. The dive site is about half a mile offshore and passengers are transferred directly to the submarine here. A surface support boat patrols the area to keep shipping away and is in constant contact with the submarine. The Canadian-built multi-million dollar wonder of high technology ensures passengers the maximum comfort being fully air conditioned while the large portholes eliminate the feeling of claustrophobia. The craft has many safety features including the fact it is naturally buoyant and is kept down by the power of its vertical thrusters. Your dive lasts about fifty minutes and a maximum depth of about 140 feet (45 m) is reached. The co-pilot gives a very informative commentary on the plant and fish life that abounds. Fantasies and fairy tales are performed before your eyes with tropical fish flittering within touching distance beyond the porthole as the sub skirts the wreck of a sunken ship. The Atlantis also makes night dives when colours change dramatically and the fish begin to follow their prey and feed. Photography is possible but you will need a high speed film (1000 ASA is recommended). Advance bookings are essential (tel. 436-8929).

Trips to other islands

Barbados's excellent air connections make the island well suited for one or two-day excursions to neighbouring islands. These could include the French island of Martinique, the beautiful tiny islands of the Grenadines or the lush tropical scenery of St Lucia. The West Indian islands are so near each other but each has its own definite character. For more details ask at your hotel reception, your representative or at any travel agency.

FIVE

Practical information for visitors

Airlines

Air Canada (Airport: 428-5077); Air Martinique (Airport: 428-4660); American Airlines (Airport: 428-4170); British Airways (B'town: 436-6413; Airport: 428-7632); BWIA (Bridgetown: 426-2111; Airport: 428-6765); Caribbean Airways (Airport: 428-5660); Cubana Airlines (see BWIA for reservations); Eastern Airlines (Airport: 428-7434); Guyana Airways (Bridgetown: 436-6224); LIAT (Bridgetown: 436-6224; Airport: 428-98937). Pan Am (Bridgetown: 436-1854; Airport: 428-7632); Wardair (Airport: 428-3131).
Remember to make/confirm your return/onward booking as soon as possible after arrival.

Banks

Barbados has an excellent banking network with head offices located in Bridgetown (usually in Broad Street) and branches in Speightstown, Holetown, Oistins and some of the large shopping plazas. Banking hours vary a little from bank to bank but most are open from 9.00 am to 3.00 pm Mondays to Thursdays, and Fridays from 9.00 am to 1.00 pm and 3 pm to 5 pm. Barclays and the Royal Bank of Canada open at 8.00 am and the Royal Bank is open from 8.00 am to 5 pm on Fridays. The Bank of Credit and Commerce is open on Saturday mornings from 9 am to 1 pm. Those wishing to change currency at the airport will find a bureau de change open from 8.00 a.m. to midnight daily.

The national currency is the Barbados dollar which is pegged to the US dollar at the rate US$1 = BDS$1.98. Many restaurants, stores and hotels will also accept US currency, either cash or traveller's cheques. Sterling can be exchanged at banks or hotels although the exchange rate at the latter is a little less favourable. Major credit cards (American Express, Visa, Access/Mastercard, Diners) are accepted at many establishments.

Books and newspapers

British, American and foreign newspapers and magazines are readily available at hotel shops and some stores where the reader will also find a selection of books. Book prices are generally higher than at home due to transport and distribution costs. If you are looking for a well-stocked bookstore, especially for Carribean editions, you can try the Cloister Bookstore in Hincks Street, Bridgetown.

Local tourist events are reported in the free newpapers *The Visitor* and *The Sunseeker*, which are published weekly and fortnightly respectively and are available in hotel lobbies, restaurants and tourist offices.

As far as local newspapers are concerned Barbados has two dailies: *The Advocate* and *The Nation*. There is also a monthly publication called *The Bajan*.

Driving licence

If you wish to drive in Barbados you must register with the authorities to obtain a temporary driving registration certificate (valid 12 months). This can be obtained directly from car hire offices or at the police stations in Hastings, Holetown and Worthing as well as Licensing Authority offices in Oistins, Bridgetown and Folkestone. You must produce your national or International Driving Permit to obtain registration and the cost of the operation is BDS$10.

Electricity

The island has a reliable supply of electrical power at 110 volts AC, 50 cycles. Sockets take standard American plugs. You should make sure that any appliances you wish to use are dual voltage and that you have the necessary adapter. Some of the larger hotels can often supply transformers.

It is quite a common practice in the smaller hotels to meter air conditioning units and in this case you usually have to purchase tokens at the reception desk.

Embassies

The addresses of the British and Canadian High Commissions and the US Embassy are indicated below. Other nationals should consult the Barbados telephone directory under 'Embassies' or 'Consulates'.

British High Commission Barclays Bank Building, Roebuck Street, Bridgetown, tel. 436-6694.

Canadian High Commission Bishop Court Hill, St Michael, tel. 429-3550

US Embassy Trident House, Broad Street, Bridgetown, tel. 436-6300.

Medical facilities

The island boasts one of the highest standards of health care in the region and has developed a National Health system that is the envy of some of its smaller neighbours. The main hospital is the 600-bed Queen Elizabeth Hospital complex near Bridgetown while clinics and health centres can be found in other parts of the island. Emergency treatment is free at the hospital but in any case it is recommended to take out a good medical insurance policy before leaving home.

Should you need a doctor or dentist during your stay your hotel will normally be able to recommend one, otherwise you will find a list in the 'Yellow Pages'.

Barbadian pharmacies are well stocked and are found in all the main towns as well as the shopping malls. However, if you are taking prescription drugs it is advisable to make sure you have an adequate supply before leaving home as not all British medicines are available.

Pests and dangers

You will not find any dangerous animals or poisonous snakes on the island, however you should be aware of the following pests and dangers:

- Mosquitoes and sandflies come into their own at sunset. Make sure you have a good repellent and maybe an anti-histamine cream. Running your air conditioner before going to bed will also reduce the risk, mosquitoes don't like the cold!
- Sea urchins can be extremely painful if you put your foot on them. The local treatment consists of disinfecting with lime juice and then rubbing on grease and heating to draw out the splinters. From personal experience I would advise you to contact the Casualty Department at the hospital.
- Manchineel trees are found on some beaches - in the more tourist beaten areas they are identifiable by the red ring painted on the trunk. The manchineel 'apples' (they look like crab apples) are poisonous and should not even be touched as they can blister the skin very badly. Do not shelter from the rain under a manchineel tree as even the water dripping off the fruit will burn your skin.
- Take reasonable precautions with your belongings. Lock any valuables in the hotel safe and don't invite 'beach bums' into your rooms.
- The sun deserves and demands your respect. Take great care with tanning, especially in the first few days. Use good quality high protection-factor sun screens and avoid sunbathing between 11 and 3 o'clock. Remember that although the temperature may be no higher than in a Mediterranean resort Barbados is much nearer the Equator and the sun can burn you even on a cloudy day or through light clothing.
- Swimming can be very dangerous on the east and south east coasts owing to the waves and undercurrents. Only swim at approved places on these coasts.

Postal services

Barbados boasts an excellent postal service with post offices to be found in all parishes of the island. You can purchase stamps and mail your correspondence at your hotel. The current postage rates to Europe are 75 cents for an airmail letter and 50 cents for a postcard. Rates to the US and Canada are 65 cents and 45 cents respectively. It usually takes about 5 to 7 days for an airmail letter to reach the UK. An express delivery service guaranteeing delivery in London or New York within 48 hours is also available.

Public holidays

The standard public holidays are New Year's Day, Good Friday, Easter Monday, Whit Monday, Christmas Day and Boxing Day. The island also celebrates May Day (first Monday in May), Kadooment Day (first Monday in August), United Nations Day (first Monday in October) and Independence Day (30th November).

Radio and television

There are four local radio stations: CBC 900 AM, Liberty 98.1 FM, Voice of Barbados 790 AM, BBS 90.7 FM. In addition there is a Rediffusion system. CBC retransmits the BBC World Service news several times a day and BBC World Service programmes can be picked up with a short-wave receiver. The island has one TV station on Channel 9. Satellite television from the United States and home videos are very popular.

Telephones

The island has a good telephone service both for local calls and international ones. Local calls from private homes or hotels are free but cost 25 cents if made from a public box. The modern telecommunications system at Bath ensures Barbados has easy access to the world and direct dialling is available to almost all countries. The cheapest way to make an international call is to reverse charges (collect call). The dialing code for calling the UK from Barbados is 01144 while if you wish to phone Barbados from the UK the international plus country code is 0101809. For those calling from the States the area code is 809.

Tipping

Most hotels and restaurants include a 10 per cent service charge in their bills. If this is not included it is usual to offer a 10-15 per cent tip. Even if service is included you may wish to add a small extra tip if you feel the service merits it. It is common to tip the chamber maids a few dollars per week. Most taxi-drivers are self-employed and only expect a tip when they have offered a long tour.

Tourist information

The Barbados Tourist Board's head office is located at Harbour Road, near the Deep Water Harbour (tel. 427-2623) where the staff are always willing to offer you their courteous assistance. The Board also has offices at the Deep Water Harbour to assist cruise ship passengers (tel. 426-1716) and at Grantley Adams International Airport (tel. 428-5012).

Water supply

Barbados is very proud of its abundant supply of pure drinking water. The island's limestone cap acts as a natural filter ensuring high quality water straight from the tap. Imported bottled mineral water is also available but expensive.

A banana 'tree' seen with fruit at the Flower Forest (St Joseph). Barbados imports much of its tropical fruit from its wetter and more fertile neighbours.

SIX

Food, drink and dining out

Introduction to Barbadian food

Bajans love their food and they like it in big portions. While Barbadian cooking does not offer the sophistication of the French West Indies, there are still plenty of specialities worth trying. Obviously the best place to sample this is in a Bajan home, but there is an increasing number of restaurants that are offering Bajan dishes on their menus and eating houses such as Brown Sugar and Kingsley Club are famous for their island fare. Bajan buffets are a popular feature in many restaurants, even those that normally offer international cuisine.

Like most local specialities Bajan dishes are based on the staple ingredients: corn meal (coo coo), plantains, breadfruit, sweet potatoes, yams and eddoes are there to fill you up while meat is usually limited to chicken, pig's trotters and other cheap cuts. Fish, especially flying fish, is very important in the local diet.

Let us now look at some of the more popular dishes:

Coo coo (sometimes spelt cou-cou or even cuckoo) is a sort of corn meal porridge, very similar to Italian 'polenta'. The skill in making it consists in the constant stirring to make sure that there are no lumps. In his novel *In The Castle of My Skin* George Lamming describes the pleasure of watching his mother prepare cuckoo and ochroes to be served with flying fish: 'The colours were in sharp contrast. Yellow and pink and the green of the sliced ochroes. When you cut it the steam flew up so that the colours became indistinct. The steam rose like a white cloud over everything, and you waited till it passed and the colours of the cuckoo came out again. The flying fish were a separate dish. You had to mix them later. She had the fish buckled in a plate and in the small blue bowl the seasoned gravy in which the fish had soaked. With the wings and head removed the fish looked much smaller than usual. But these weren't wasted. The wings and head with the back and side bones were boiled and eaten on another occasion.'

Flying fish were very much the poor man's fish but they have remained the national dish, even if at times they are in short demand. Other more expensive and delicious fish are often offered in the island's restaurants and include king fish, red snapper and dolphin (which is not our friend the mammal). 'Sea eggs' (sea urchins) are also a speciality when in season and when it is legally permitted to collect them.

Another Bajan favourite is **pudding and souse.** The pudding consists of well-seasoned grated sweet potato steamed in the intestine of a pig, sausage-fashion. This is served with 'souse', i.e. pork that has been cooked and then pickled with lime juice, hot pepper, cucumber, onion and other ingredients.

Other specialities include pepperpot (a type of spicy stew), peas and rice, macaroni pie and conkies (a spicy coconut and cornmeal mix steamed in plantain leaves). Bajan sweets would include delicious coconut pies and banana bread.

As many visitors find these traditional Barbadian dishes a little too different from their normal eating habits, in recent years many restaurateurs have developed what has become known as 'nu Bajan cuisine' which is essentially a blend of international cooking dressed up in local exotic ingredients, such as garnishes, dressings and sauces containing coconut, guava, rum, ginger and pineapple, to name but a few.

Tropical fruit

The first-time visitor to the tropics will of course find a bewildering array of tropical fruit and vegetables, although it should be remembered that Barbados is not a great fruit producer and much is imported from neighbouring islands. Here is a short description of some of the fruit and vegetables you might find (remember that some are available only at certain times of the year):

Bananas will certainly need no introduction, but look out for the small stubby ones that are called 'figs'. Secondly try not to confuse **plantains** with bananas — easy you may say, but it is surprising how many people confuse them. Plantains, which are used as vegetables, come in two colours — green and yellow — so don't be tricked into thinking that everything yellow is a banana. The yellow plantains are in fact sweetish and can be eaten without cooking but the secret for distinguishing a banana from a plantain is that the latter is more angular. Look carefully at a green plantain and then look around you at the yellow 'banana-like' ware, you'll soon learn to spot the difference. By the way, the plantain is one of the staple products in the West Indian diet and can be prepared in many different ways. Try cutting one up into thin slices and frying them and you'll end up with delicious chips!

Papaya (also called pawpaw in the West Indies) is the fruit that Columbus described as the 'fruit of the angels' and was the mainstay of the Amerindian diet. This melon-like fruit grows up the stem of the tree. The fruit can vary in size (up to 4 kilograms) and shape (elongated or round) and are yellowish-orange when ripe. Inside you will find many dark seeds buried in the flesh. Like melons the taste can vary very much and sometimes you'll get a rather tasteless marrow-like specimen. Papaya is often served at breakfast with a little **lime** juice squeezed over it.

Mangoes are one of the commonest fruits on the island. The fruit can vary in colour according to the variety and stage of ripeness, but if the skin is yellowish or pinkish the fruit is ready to eat. You can also try green mangoes as a salad, dressed with a little lime juice.

Originally the small green citrus fruit known as the **lime** came from Asia but today it is one of the basic ingredients of West Indian cookery. Of course that deliciously refreshing Caribbean lime-juice cordial is known far beyond the borders of the region. Perhaps less known, but none the less useful, is that in an emergency lime juice can be used as a disinfectant.

Another fruit that is commonly used to make drinks is the **soursop**. This is a large dark green oval-shaped fruit with a spiny surface. The whitish flesh inside can be eaten or sieved for juice or cream. Make sure the fruit is really ripe before opening it.

Several tropical fruits are probably more appreciated in the jam or jelly form than fresh and the **guava** is the classic example. This small yellowish pear-shaped fruit has a pinkish flesh that is full of small seeds.

If you see a reddish brown pine-cone-like fruit about the size of a small apple, then you are looking at a **sugar apple.** It has a sweet granular pulp with a custard-like consistency — in fact in some Caribbean countries it is called the custard apple.

Perhaps no fruit tree more symbolises an idyllic Caribbean beach that the coconut palm and one of the delights for the visitor is tasting this fruit in its various stages of development. If you are thirsty nothing can beat the thirst-quenching 'water' of the green

A breadfruit tree at St Nicholas Abbey. The breadfruit was introduced to the West Indies by Captain Bligh (of **Mutiny on the Bounty** *fame) as 'slave fodder'.*

coconut while if you are hungry then the brown one will give you plenty to chew on. Something in between? Then ask the seller to give you a green coconut that has ripened enough to form jelly inside.

If you hear someone speaking about 'pears' in Barbados, then inevitably they are speaking about the familiar **avocado.** Watch the calories because they have a very high fat content!

Breadfruit trees can be spotted growing in the wild everywhere and this plentiful fruit that looks like a green football is a West Indian staple. It was imported to the region from the South Pacific by Captain Bligh (of *Mutiny on the Bounty* fame) to provide food for the plantation slaves. The taste is somewhat similar to potato and it can be cooked in many different ways.

Island drinks

Naturally **rum** is the national drink on this sugar-producing island and it is a tradition that goes back to the earliest pioneer days. It is cheap and is served in an infinite variety of cocktails and punches as well as neat. You will find white and dark varieties available but most Bajans drink the latter. **Falernum** is a local liqueur made from rum, lime juice, sugar and almond essence.

Imported spirits are also on sale but you should be prepared for high prices as the Government slaps import duties on such luxuries.

Beer drinkers will have reasons to rejoice at the good news that Banks Breweries of Barbados produces an excellent lager whose popularity has surpassed this island's shores and is known throughout the Caribbean region.

As far as local soft drinks are concerned **mauby** and **sorrel** are the two favourites. The former is a cordial made from the bark of a tree and tastes somewhat like aniseed. Sorrel, on the other hand, is made from the red sepals of the sorrel plant. This is the traditional Barbadian Christmas drink although you will find it on sale throughout the year.

Restaurants

The visitor will find a wide selection of restaurants reflecting all tastes and catering for most pockets. In general, however, you should be prepared to pay more than for a similar meal in Britain. Many foodstuffs are imported and this is reflected in menu prices.

Most restaurants offer light lunches at reasonable prices but dinners can be considerably more expensive. Typical table d'hôte dinners cost around BDS$50 and à la carte main courses are in the BDS$25-40 range in the better known establishments. Restaurants charge a 5 per cent Government sales tax and usually add 10 per cent for service to your bill. Below you will find a selection of some of the island's many restaurants.

St Peter, St James and St Thomas
Chrizel's Garden Gibbes, St Peter, tel. 422-2403. Attractive small restaurant open only for dinner. Closed Sundays. Bajan vegetarian cuisine.

La Piperade Glitter Bay Hotel, St James, tel. 422-4111. Elegant restaurant in top 'Gold Coast' resort. International cuisine. Mondays and Fridays are buffet and barbecue evenings respectively with floorshows and dancing.

La Cage aux Folles Paynes Bay, St James, tel. 432-1203. Offers a blend of French and Chinese cooking.

Il Portico Sandy Lane, St James, tel. 432-1311. Elegant Italian restaurant in the island's top hotel.

Koko's Prospect, St James, tel. 424-4557. Bajan and 'Nu Bajan' cuisine at reasonable prices. Specialities include island rabbit with a tamarind and ginger sauce and stuffed crabs.

Folkestone Beach Restaurant Folkestone, St James. A casual and inexpensive eating house near Folkestone Beach, open for lunch and dinner. Local specialities.

Bagatelle Great House Highway 2A, St Thomas, tel. 425-0666. One of the island's top restaurants in beautiful old plantation house which once belonged to a seventeenth-century Governor of Barbados, Lord Willoughby. To reach the restaurant from the west coast, turn inland at the church in Holetown and then turn right at St Thomas Parish Church onto Highway 2A. Arriving from the south take Highway 2A off the ring road. International cuisine.

Bridgetown and St Michael
Fisherman's Wharf Careenage, Bridgetown, tel. 436-7778. Right on the waterfront with nice view of town. Well known for its fish dishes. Excellent moderately-priced lunches. Bajan dishes.

Brown Sugar Aquatic Gap, St Michael, tel. 427-76854. Located not far from the Hilton Hotel, opposite Garrison Savannah. Very popular with Bridgetown businessmen at lunchtime. One of the island's best restaurants for Bajan food. Excellent lunch buffets at moderate prices.

Ribiera Black Rock, St Michael, tel. 424-7859. Located near Spring Garden roundabout. Ribiera offers Caribbean specialities as well as grills. Special three course dinner offer includes free transport.

Fort Charles Grill Hilton Hotel, St Michael, tel. 426-0200. International and local cooking in one of the island's top resorts.

Peter the Fisherman Island Inn, St Michael, tel.426-0057. Located at Aquatic Gap near the Hilton Hotel. A moderately priced restaurant offering good value. Bajan and international cuisine.

Christ Church

Joseph's St Lawrence Gap, Christ Church. International cooking in what is considered one of the best restaurants on the island.

Suzie Yong St Lawrence Gap, Christ Church, tel. 428-1865. Chinese restaurant located in the heart of the lively south coast.

Boomer's St Lawrence Gap, Christ Church, tel. 428-8439. Very popular and moderately priced restaurant and bar. Informal atmosphere and friendly staff combined with good value food.

Da Luciano Hastings, Christ Church, tel. 427-5518. One of the island's leading Italian restaurants set in a building of architectural interest. Classical Italian cuisine, famous for its filetto battuto alla Luciano (flambéed beef fillet, sautéed in butter with mustard, mushrooms and cream).

Pisces St Lawrence, Christ Church, tel. 426-4668. One of the top restaurants if you are looking for fish dishes. Romantic setting over St Lawrence Bay. Evenings only. Booking recommended.

Ocean View Hastings, Christ Church, tel. 427-7821. One of the oldest hotels on the island, once a favourite haunt of Ernest Hemingway. Offers typical Bajan fare.

St Philip

Sunbury Plantation House Sunbury, St Philip, tel. 423-6270. Lovely plantation house setting. Nice lunches available in the shady courtyard at reasonable prices. Exclusive dinners arranged once a week when you will be the personal guests of the owners, drinks and transport included in the price.

Pavilion Crane Beach, St Philip, tel. 423-6220. Fashionable restaurant offering excellent seafood, set on a low cliff overlooking one of the most beautiful beaches on Barbados (the beach is even floodlit for evening diners). Live entertainment every night.

Cobbler's Reef Sam Lord's Castle, St Philip, tel. 423-7350. One of the restaurants on the the premises of this large resort. International fare. Dinners only. Sam Lord's Castle is also famous for its weekly Bajan Fiesta set in a reproduced Bajan village.

St Joseph

Kingsley Club Cattlewash, St Joseph, tel. 433-9422. A fine colonial-style inn set on the East Coast Road. A favourite eating spot at lunch-time for those touring the island. Excellent Barbadian food served on the breezy verandah. For starters try the fish chowder with home-baked bread!

Atlantis Hotel Bathsheba, St Joseph, tel. 433-9445. Popular lunch-time port of call at spectacular Tent Bay. Bajan food at moderate prices.

Information for self-caterers

Self-catering is very popular on Barbados and a large number of hotels offer kitchen facilities. Shopping is certainly no problem in most places as you will find mini-markets and supermarkets at hand offering a wide selection of imported foodstuffs. Generally speaking prices are above those in the UK owing to the high cost of importing food. One thing you will not find, however, is the greengrocer's, and you may well be disappointed in the selection of fruit and vegetables available in the supermarket. If you are looking for fresh fruit and vegetables you will have to go into town and shop at Fairchild or Cheapside markets, a colourful experience in itself. For those staying in the north, Speightstown too offers its 'hucksters' with their piles of yams, plantains and avocados on the pavement. Fresh fish can be bought at the fish markets in Bridgetown, Oistins and Speightstown, while frozen fish is available in the supermarkets.

Another feature of Barbados that self-caterers will appreciate is the abundance of 'takeaways'. If you are staying on the west or south coasts you will have no difficulty in finding an outlet for takeaway fried chicken, pizza or 'roti' (a sort of pancake filled with meat and vegetables).

SEVEN

The sporting life

The Barbados Board of Tourism has recognised that sport on this pleasant island is not only a matter for the locals but is a factor that attracts visitors. To promote sport-oriented tourism it has appointed a Sports Consultant — at present no less a personality than one of the world's most famous cricketers, Sir Gary Sobers. Besides offering excellent facilities to the individual sportsperson, the Tourist Board can arrange matches for visiting teams in a whole range of events. Below you will find outlined the island's main facilities.

Water sports

Naturally on a tropical island you would expect water sports to have a key role, and on Barbados you will not be disappointed. The island's gently sloping west and south-west coasts with their lovely sandy beaches offer excellent opportunities for **swimming** and **snorkelling.** Many of the more popular beaches have life-guards and safe swimming areas are marked off with buoys. Hotels and diving firms rent out snorkelling gear for those who have not brought their own. Particular care should be taken to protect the body against the strong rays of the sun (a T-shirt is recommended for the first days) and on some beaches you should watch out for sea urchins lurking on the sea bottom — a foot full of their painful spines can ruin your holiday. In general swimming is not recommended on the south-east and east coasts owing to the pounding surf and dangerous currents, although there are one or two safe bathing spots such as Bath Bay.

Scuba and **skin diving** enthusiasts will find Barbados offers good opportunities off the west and south coasts, with fringe and patch reefs for shallow dives and barrier reefs averaging 20-30 metre (60-100 feet) tops. Near Holetown there is Folkestone Underwater Park where underwater trails have been prepared round the coral reef that lies about a kilometre off shore. The big attraction here is the wreck of the freighter *Stravronika* which was sunk here some years ago to attact marine fauna and flora. The tug *Berwyn* in Carlisle Bay, barely a few feet below the surface, offers a good site for beginners and snorkellers. You will find plenty of support boats willing to take you out to the reef and rent you equipment. The firm Exploresub Barbados, St Lawrence Gap, Christ Church (tel. 428-3504) offers good facilities with two 30-foot boats and professionally trained staff. Non-divers are welcome to try an introductory course.

Sailing is popular everywhere and you find plenty of catamarans, Hobie Cats and Sunfish for hire along the west and south coast beaches with the gentle trade winds assuring excellent conditions. The breezier south coast has become an important **windsurfing** centre and the 1983 Mistral World Championships were held here. For details of windsurf hire and instruction, contact The Barbados Windsurfing Club, Maxwell, Christ Church (tel. 428-9095). **Surfing** too has become popular on the Atlantic coast near North Point (St Lucy) and at Bathsheba (St Joseph). Surfing championships are held at Bathsheba in November, but you have to be really good to beat the local boys.

The placid waters of the west coast, on the other hand, attract motorised water sports such as **water skiing, parasailing** and **jetskiing.** Some of the more expensive hotels offer free water sports but if you are staying elsewhere you will find no shortage of facilities. The Cunard Paradise Beach Hotel, for example, offers packages for water sports enthusiasts, where for an all-inclusive rate you can enjoy four hours of water sports and parasailing.

Cricket

Cricket is the Bajan national sport par excellence and if you want to see an exciting game of cricket there is no better place, whether it be on a village green or at Bridgetown's Kensington Oval. International test matches are played between January and April while summer visitors can enjoy First Division sport from May to Mid-December. And if you and a few friends fancy a game yourselves it shouldn't be too difficult to arrange, just ask around and you won't be disappointed for long!

Fishing

The island offers the angler good sport, especially off the northern and southern coasts where the placid waters of the Caribbean meet the ocean currents. Here the big game fishermen will find blue marlin (more plentiful in winter), wahoo, dolphin (not the mammal!), king fish and barracuda. Coastal fishermen who wish to troll from a small boat can expect to find bonito, king fish, barracuda, mackerel and snapper. Bottom fishing is popular over the reefs, your catch may include snapper, chubb and barracuda, while small barracuda, yellowtail, jacks and tarpon can be caught by casting from rocks or wading out a short distance.

Small boats for trolling can be hired by enquiring at water sports firms along the west coast, while those interested in deep sea fishing may contact operators such as Blue Jay Charters (422-2098) or Jolly Roger Water Sports (432-7090).

Golf

The island boasts three golf courses: Sandy Lane, Rockley and Heywoods. Sandy Lane has an 18-hole international standards course on the inland side of Highway 1 near Holetown. The 54-hole Barbados Amateur Open Golf Tournament is held here in October and attracts amateurs from all over the world. Several tour operators offer stays at the Sandy Lane Hotel combined with a golfing holiday, but naturally non-residents are welcome too. For bookings call 432-1145.

The Rockley Resort Golf Club is especially popular with those staying near Bridgetown or on the south coast. It is conveniently located at Rockley, just south of the capital, off Highway 7, and offers an attractive 9-hole course in very pleasant surroundings. For bookings telephone 427-5890.

Finally the Heywoods Resort (tel. 422-4900) in St. Peter offers a 9-hole 'pitch and putt' course for those staying in the north.

Hiking

The beautiful rugged coastlines of the north, the east and the south-east, Hackleton's Cliff with its spectacular views and the hilly Scotland District all make exciting hiking country. Try to get an early start and avoid the hottest hours of the day and don't forget to take plenty of sunscreen, a hat and of course your camera. Several organised walking tours are offered. The Outdoor Club of Barbados (tel. 436-5328) offer full-day excursions that include a five-mile hike to the hidden beauty spots of the east coast, meals and entertainment included. On the other hand, the National Trust has a programme of free hikes (no frills attached) on Sundays (see *The Visitor* newspaper for details of the itinerary and starting point) with a very early start.

Horse races

Second in popularity only to cricket are the races organised by the Barbados Turf Club at Garrison Savannah (St Michael) two Saturdays a month, from January to May, and August to November. You may pay for a seat in the stands or have a free show from the side-lines.

Horse-riding

There are several stables located in the parishes of St James, St Thomas and St Philip offering mounts for rides along the beaches or through the pretty rolling country of central Barbados. For those interested the following addresses may be useful: Country Corral Riding Stables, Taitt's Plantation, St James (tel. 422-2401) or Sunbury Stables, Sunbury, St Philip (tel. 423-6270).

Tennis

Many of the larger hotels have their own tennis courts for their guests and visitors. Often an extra charge is made when the courts are flood-lit. Public hard and grass courts are available at Folkestone (near St James Parish Church) and at the Garrison (St Michael).

EIGHT

Night life and entertainment

While you will not find any casinos on the island, Barbados can offer the visitor a good selection of nightlife and entertainment all year round. Of course if you are staying in one of the smaller hotels in the low season you may find little on 'at home', but rest assured there is always something on at one of the neighbouring resorts. Below you will find just some of the attractions the island can offer visitors. Remember that clubs and discos do change their management fairly frequently and their reputation can change overnight if a popular resident band decides to move on, therefore it is advisable to check with your tour representative or hotel reception about the latest situation.

Dinner shows

Dinner shows are a well-established attraction on Barbados and owe their immense success to their very high professional standards. Generally speaking the price includes transport to and from your hotel, dinner and drinks and the show. In some cases you can pay an entrance fee for drinks and the show.

'1627 and all that. . .' offers a dazzling potpourri of authentic Bajan dance and folklore by the Barbados Dance Theatre Company on Sunday and Thursday evenings in the impressive setting of the **Barbados Museum.** A unique experience of sampling the island's history in the attractive museum (once the military detention centre!) with its largely European-oriented plantocracy exhibits and this lively display of African heritage that for centuries was kept underground. The scenes include children's games, double-dealing courtship that concludes in an exciting stick fight, the maypole dance and others, all accompanied by the throbbing rhythm of the tuk band.

'Barbados, Barbados', on the other hand, is performed on Tuesday evenings at **Balls,** a former sugar estate in Christ Church. It is based on the life of Rachel Pringle, a larger-than-life character who ran a Bridgetown tavern in the eighteenth century. The tavern was a popular port of call for visiting sailors and one night in 1789 it was visited by Prince William Henry (the future William IV) and a party of officers who set about smashing the place up in drunken merriment — the next day the Prince made his amends by offering Rachel (whom he had personally unseated) generous compensation. The setting is the former boiling house on the estate and the show consists of a musical comedy.

'Tropical Spectacular II' is a colourful cabaret dinner show that is held in the garden of the **Plantation Restaurant** (St Lawrence). The company offers music, dancing and rhythms of the Caribbean with 35 dancers portraying the island's history from the Arawaks, through the years of piracy and slavery to the present day. The shows are held on Wednesdays and Fridays. The same restaurant also offers dinner shows on Mondays, Tuesdays and Fridays to the accompaniment of top bands such as Spice and The Merrymen. The Plantation Restaurant also offers the formula 'show and unlimited drinks' for those who do not wish to dine.

Calypso and steel bands

Two dominating features of Caribbean music are of course calypso and steel bands. Naturally calypso singing has moved with the times and today is an up-beat soca version rather than the Belafonte variety of yester year. Steel bands, if they are good, can offer a wonderful versatility and can play all types of music. (However, in Barbados you will not find the enormous steelband 'symphony orchestras' that exist in Trinidad and are willing to take on anything from Beethoven to Verdi.) Many of the larger hotels offer nightly entertainment in this style and the smaller properties often feature a weekly Bajan buffet or barbecue with a steel band. For details of what's on during your holiday period you should consult the free newspaper *The Visitor*. Some of the most popular night spots outside the hotels include: **Harbour Lights,** Bay Street, Bridgetown (436-7225); **The Warehouse,** Cavan's Lane, Bridgetown (436-2897)

Jazz

Jazz fans are catered for at **The Belair Jazz Club,** Bay Street, Bridgetown, where you can meet a fair cross section of Barbadian society.

Discos and pubs

For those who prefer dancing to the sound of international stars rather than dancing under the stars, the island can offer such hot spots as **Club Miliki** (Heywoods Resort, near Speightstown), **Apple Experience** at Hastings and **After Day Disco** at St Lawrence.

The local version of the British pub is the the the Barbadian rum shop where you may enjoy a cheap drink, local chit chat and maybe a game of dominoes in rudimentary surroundings. Those who long for a British-style pub in the tropics may like to try **The Ship Inn** at St Lawrence (south coast) or its sister establishment, **The Coach House** at Paynes Bay, near Holetown.

Cinema and theatre

There are a number of cinemas in the Bridgetown area. For details of programmes consult the local newspapers. Theatre performances are given in the theatre in **Queen's Park** and the **Frank Collymore Hall** in town. Many of the shows are comedy packed with Bajan dialect so the visitor is unlikely to catch the punch lines — if you wish to try the experience, check the local newspapers for details.

Festivals

Fun-loving Bajans have dotted their calendar with festivals that attract the locals and visitors alike. There are four major ones:
- **The Holetown Festival** takes place in February to celebrate the landing of the first permanent settlers on 17 February, 1627. Celebrations include a blend of old and new, with mediaeval songs sung in churches, folksongs, calypso beat and dancing in the streets, street markets and fairs.
- **Oistins Fish Festival** in April gives the inhabitants of this fishing town the opportunity to show off their traditional skills in such

events as boat racing, fishing and fish-boning. The town is enlivened by steel bands and street dancing while visitors can try out Bajan dishes on sale in the many little stalls.

- **Crop Over Festival** is what Carnival is to Trinidad and is held from mid-July and lasts until Kadooment Day (the first Monday in August). Crop Over celebrates the completion of the cane harvest (which in fact is over by June) and is marked by such events as the Calypso Contest which offers the much coveted title of Calypso Monarch of the Year. The climax comes on Kadooment Day when masquerading bands begin their road march from the National Stadium to Spring Garden Highway. All of Barbados seems to be there, either in the parade or just watching and joining in the fun.

- **The National Independence Festival** of the Creative Arts shows the more serious side of the Bajan character, when Barbadians of all age groups pit their talents in a variety of events such as writing, music, singing, acting and dancing. The festival coincides with the celebration of Independence Day on 30 November.

A tuk band offers entertainment at a Bajan dinner show. The whistle and drums derive from British military bands — the rhythm no.

NINE

Shopping and souvenirs

Facilities and hours of business

Barbados offers some of the best shopping facilities in the Caribbean with modern department stores in Bridgetown and shopping plazas scattered here and there along the coast. Many of the larger hotel complexes too have branches of Bridgetown stores. Most department stores in town are open from 8 am to 4 pm and are closed on Saturday afternoons. Shops and supermarkets in tourist areas are generally open longer.

Duty-free shopping

You will find a wide array of imported luxury goods, ranging from Japanese cameras to Irish crystal, available at duty-free prices. To purchase goods in island stores at duty-free prices the visitor must produce his/her travel document and airline ticket. The original and duplicate of the sales invoice is attached to the travel ticket. On departure the invoice must be presented to the immigration officer. Certain categories of goods can be collected when purchased, others are delivered to the airport or harbour pick-up point (after going through customs). Goods included in the second category include spirits, wines, cigarettes, video equipment, televisions and home computers. If you wish to have the goods delivered to the airport or the harbour make sure you make your purchase in good time. For many a more convenient system of buying duty-free cigarettes or drinks is to purchase them directly at the airport and harbour facilities.

Remember, however, that on many items (duty-free or not) you will be expected to pay customs duties when you arrive home. At present UK residents (over the age of 17) are permitted to bring in duty-free up to one litre of spirits, 200 cigarettes, 50 grammes (two fluid ounces) of perfume and £32 worth of other goods. US residents must pay duty on goods exceeding US$400 retail value in the country of purchase while up to one quart of liquor is duty-free for persons over 21. Canadians, on the other hand, may claim up to Can. $300 per year exemption on goods, provided that the trip exceeded seven days. The exemption may include 40 oz. of alcoholic beverages, 50 cigars, 200 cigarettes and two pounds of tobacco. The age limit for exemption on alcohol depends on the regulations of the province where you clear customs.

Souvenirs

Island souvenirs may vary from T-shirts and jewellery purchased (after long bargaining) from the beach boys or the beach markets and handicrafts made from straw and wood. If you are in the Deep Water Harbour area you might like to try the attractive stalls and boutiques of Pelican Village on Princess Alice Highway. Looking for something inexpensive but original? — then the simple but handsome pottery of Chalky Mount can make an interesting souvenir, as can the leather and wooden goods made and sold by Rasta craftsmen in Temple Yard, Bridgetown.

Island artist Jill Walker produces a collection of very attractive prints, corkbacked place mats, hand screenprinted material and other attractive souvenirs which are sold in a chain of shops known as the 'Best of Barbados'. You will find them at: the Sandpiper Inn (Holetown); Mall 34, Broad Street, Bridgetown; Southern Palms Hotel, (St Lawrence Gap); Sam Lord's Castle; Keswick (Hastings) and the Flower Forest (Richmond).

TEN

About the island

The island's geography

Unlike its neighbours in the Eastern Caribbean, Barbados is not part of the Caribbean Volcanic Arc, lying in fact 95 miles to the east of its nearest neighbour, St Vincent. Situated at latitude 13°N and longitude 59°W it is the most easterly of all the Caribbean islands, a feature that will play a major role in its history. Barbados is a small island, only 21 miles (33 kms) long and 14 miles (22 kms) across at its widest point, with a total area of 166 square miles (430 sq kms). Seen from above the island has been compared in shape to a leg of mutton, with the narrow end in the north.

Compared to many of its volcanic neighbours Barbados is relatively flat or at most hilly, with the land rising in terraces to its highest point at Mount Hillaby, 1,115 feet (337 m) in the centre of the island. These terraces were produced during the Ice Age by earth movements and the changing sea level. Geologically Barbados is composed of a thick layer of coral sandwiched between a thin topsoil and an alluvial base of sandstone and clay that was deposited on the Caribbean floor over millions of years by the great rivers of South America.

The island may be divided into three main topographical areas: the Scotland District in the north east, a rugged hilly area which was formed where the coral cap has been eroded away by tidal waves; an upland plateau which falls away to the west, south west and south of the Scotland District marked by the escarpment, Hackleton's Cliff, on its eastern edge; the lowland plateau which covers the coastal areas and much of the south.

There are no real visible rivers on the island as most of the water filters through the coral cap into underground caverns and rivers. This explains place names such as River Bay and River Road where no visible river exists. On the other hand there are gullies with splendid tropical vegetation and rivers can form quickly here after heavy rain.

As far as coastline is concerned there is a stark contrast between the fine white and pink sandy beaches of the west and south-west coasts overlooking the transparent waters of the placid Caribbean, and the beautiful, rugged northern, eastern and south-eastern coasts which are exposed to the full force of the Atlantic.

Climate

Barbados has a pleasant climate throughout the year with only minimum variations in temperature between summer and winter. The island lies in the path of the north-east trade winds which guarantee a constant cooling breeze. The climate is somewhat drier than that of its neighbours with a dry season extending from January to May and a somewhat wetter summer and autumn. Relative humidity rarely exceeds 72 per cent and it often much lower, while the island's greatest attraction, the sun, shines for over 3000 hours a year.

As in most Caribbean islands there are tropical storms and the occasional hurricane. Fortunately most hurricanes seem to pass north of the island. When they occur they are most likely in the late summer and early autumn.

Max. temperatures (monthly averages) °C.

Jan	Feb	March	April	May	June	July	Aug	Sept	Oct	Nov	Dec
29	30	30	31	31	31	31	31	31	31	30	29

Average daily hours of sunshine

Jan	Feb	March	April	May	June	July	Aug	Sept	Oct	Nov	Dec
10	10	9	8	7	7	7	8	8	7	8	9

Mean monthly precipitation (mm)

Jan	Feb	March	April	May	June	July	Aug	Sept	Oct	Nov	Dec
51	25	25	38	51	100	127	152	165	165	178	76

Relative humidity %

Jan	Feb	March	April	May	June	July	Aug	Sept	Oct	Nov	Dec
67	66	65	63	63	68	70	71	71	73	73	71

Flora

Because the island is relatively flat it was easy for the first settlers to clear the original vegetation to make way for arable land. Today the only vestige of the original vegetation can be found at Turner's Hall Woods in a rather remote corner of central Barbados. Here you will find such rare trees as locust and jack-in-the-box. The strange name of the latter tree derives from the fact that it bears a fruit with a hollow pod and the seed which stands vertically inside pops out through a hole at the top. The spiny macaw palm too can be found in this remote part of the island. Look out for fallen trunks because a thorn in the foot can be very painful. Elsewhere imported trees, both for timber and fruit, can be found, the most common examples being casuarina, mahogany and mango.

Whatever the season you will find beautiful tropical plants and trees in bloom throughout the year: oleanders, hibiscus, ginger lilies, Ixora, just to name a few. In winter you will see a profusion of bougainvilleas and poinsettias, while the spring showers bring out bignonias and frangipani. The summer visitor will enjoy the bright red blossom of the flamboyant, a magnificent ornamental tree that originated in Madagscar. Its crown is sometimes wider than the height of the tree. Garden lovers and botanists will certainly be impressed by the fine public and private gardens the island offers and a visit to such places as **Welchman Hall Gully, Andromeda Gardens,** the **Flower Forest** and **Turner Hall Woods** will be one of the highlights of your holiday.

Fauna

The destruction of the natural vegetation and the high percentage of arable land has meant that Barbados can offer little in fauna (apart from bird life). The two main species that do exist, the green-faced monkey and the mongoose, were both imported. The unusual green-faced monkey was imported from Africa and quickly proliferated on the island. Today it is still common in the wooded areas but is considered a nuisance by farmers because it is very destructive. Look out for them in areas such as Farley Hill, Turner Hall Woods, Welchman Hall Gully or at Francia Great House (St George). If you want to be sure of seeing them and getting some interesting photographs then you should visit the **Barbados Wildlife Reserve** (St Peter) where about fifty monkeys live in natural surroundings. The mongoose, on the other hand, was imported with a purpose in mind — to rid the sugar-cane fields of rats. The experiment was only partially successful as the rat population has not been eliminated and the mongoose has become a pest in that it attacks poultry. A resident the visitor is more likely to hear than to see is the tiny whistling frog whose piercing call can be heard at night. The brown and yellow adult frog only grows to about 2.5 cm (1 inch) long. What you will probably see hopping along the paths at night is the large bull frog which originally came from South America.

Bird watchers will find a fair variety of birds (including many migrants). The visitor is likely to be charmed by the tiny hummingbird as it darts from flower to flower or the colourful yellow breast which can commonly be seen on fruit trees. The tameness of the birds is another feature — you will find it quite usual to have a sparrow or a blackbird (not the European species) sitting on your table and stealing some sugar from the sugar basin while you are breakfasting. Winter visitors can enjoy the spectacle of roosting white egrets in the mangrove swamp of **Graeme Hall Swamp,** a bird sanctuary located just a few minutes' walk off the busy Highway 7 at Worthing (Christ Church).

Communications

As far as external communications are concerned, Barbados has excellent communications with the outside world. Its two main infrastructures are Grantley Adams International Airport in the southern parish of Christ Church and the Deep Water Harbour at Bridgetown. Grantley Adams is one of the leading airports in the Caribbean with good connections to North America and Europe. Its modern facilities allow the largest jets to land in safety and passenger handling is geared to the large influx of visitors. Until about thirty years ago the Careenage in Bridgetown was the island's main port. This could only handle light inter-island traffic and larger ships had to anchor out in Carlisle Bay. The new Deep Water Harbour allows the berthing of cargo and cruise ships.

Opposite: *St Nicholas Abbey (St Peter) with its Dutch-styled gables dates from the 17th century and is one of the best examples of a Barbadian Great House.*

Barbados has been able to take advantage of the advent of high tech for its telecommunications centre on the east coast permits immediate access to satellite communications. This has stimulated the setting up of offshore financial services and data processing.

Internal communications too are probably the best of any East Caribbean island. Barbadian roadbuilders have been helped by the relatively flat terrain and today even the most remote village is connected to Bridgetown by paved road. The road system consists of a radial highway network with spokes to the north, east and south from Bridgetown. Secondary roads then link up the highways to ensure a capillary network. In recent years a new highway has been built from the airport to the west coast and forms an efficient ring road round the capital.

The economy

Unlike some of its other Caribbean neighbours, Barbados has managed to ride out the economic crises that have hit the region in the 1980s. It has managed to notch up a constant annual growth rate, in real terms, of about two and a half per cent. Nothing particularly exciting at first sight, but it has been the ability to maintain this steady growth that has pushed the per capita income (in Gross Domestic Product terms) to US$5,795 (1988 figures), not only one of the highest in the Caribbean, but one which compares favourably with some of the poorer areas of Western Europe. Like many developing countries, unemployment is a chronic problem, with about 18 per cent of the labour force without work. To make any real impact on this figure, politicians estimate that a 6-7 per cent annual growth rate would be necessary.

The local economy is based on three pillars: tourism, light manufacturing and agriculture, which account for about 14 per cent, 13 per cent and 7 per cent respectively of the Gross Domestic Product. In the last twenty years there has been a real turn-about in these figures, for example in 1970 tourism accounted for only 9 per cent of the GDP while sugar alone made up 9.2 per cent (compared with 3.9 per cent today). Manufacturing industry, on the

Opposite: *A view over the rugged east coastline, still untouched by tourism.*

other hand, has experienced its ups-and-downs, with a particularly bad spell in the mid-1980s when the US electroncis firm Intel decided to close its Barbados plant with the loss of one thousand jobs.

Tourism

First of all the sector that affects the visitor directly, tourism. In 1988 the number of visitors to the island exceeded 450,000, no mean feat for such a small nation, and directly or indirectly provided employment for between 15,000 and 20,000 Barbadians (statistics in this section are by no means unanimous). Visitors arriving by air during daylight hours can realise the extent of tourism before even putting foot on Barbadian soil, for as the plane follows the south coast before its approach to Grantley Adams International Airport, the traveller will notice the numerous hotels and holdiay appartments of all shapes and styles — but fortunately no high-rise development — that follow Highway 7 south from Bridgetown, through the suburbs of Hastings, Rockley and Worthing to the famous St Lawrence Gap, with its proliferation of hotels, restaurants and discos, and beyond to Maxwell, before petering out at Oistins. And this is just part of the scene, the lively south coast that mainly caters for the lower end of the market. Well-heeled travellers may be destined for Barbados's famous 'Gold Coast' or 'Platinum Coast', according to taste, in the parishes of St James and St Peter. It is here that we find the luxury of resorts such as Sandy Lane, the Royal Pavilion and a conspicuous number of well organised first class hotels. Most of the larger resorts belong to multi-national concerns such as Cunard, Hilton, Trusthouse Forte, but there are also examples of large-scale resorts built by the Barbados Government (Heywoods, St Peter) and entrusted to private management, and several owner-managed smaller properties. Although most of the development started in the 1960s, Barbados has a long tradition as a vacation island. Already in the eighteenth century it was well known for its salubrious climate, George Washington's brother being one of its better known convalescent patients. The nineteenth century saw the establishment of the Crane Hotel on the south-east coast and the small Atlantis Hotel at Bathsheba. Both are still very much alive and are particularly popular with Barbadians who wish to leave the bustle and heat of Bridgetown.

Some Barbadians think that the economy is overdependent on tourism, and indeed the tourist market is highly fickle. The

Barbados dollar is pegged to the US dollar and any variation of the exchange rate between the dollar and European currencies can make a considerable difference to the number of European visitors to the island. Traditionally Caribbean destinations have been winter destinations for North Americans and Europeans who wish to escape the rigour of a cold winter; however, in recent years, the Tourist Board has been trying, with some success, to promote holidays on the island in other seasons. The summer months are now becoming increasingly popular with visitors who enjoy the advantages of low season prices and better service.

Farley Hill Home. The remains of what was one of the most sumptuous Great Houses on the island. The film Island in the sun *was shot here. A few years later the house was destroyed by fire. Now it is part of the Farley Hill National Park.*

Manufacturing

Perhaps this is the sector that most surprises visitors. The Caribbean is usually associated with tourism, perhaps agriculture, but hardly manufacturing. First of all, rest assured that there is no heavy industry that is likely to cause pollution and spoil the beaches. With the exception of the cement plant, industry is limited to light, labour-intensive sectors, such as clothing, electronics and food-processing. Development in this sector is hindered by access to suitable markets and the relatively high cost of labour in Barbados. To guarantee an economy of scale, Barbados must export, but where? The island has some outlet in the US market under President Reagan's much heralded Caribbean Basin Initiative, but in fact the small islands of the Eastern Caribbean, which were considered so vitally important to US policy, received only a tiny proportion of investment funds. Furthermore, protectionist moves by US manufacturers have hindered the import of garments from the Caribbean. The alternative market is Barbados's East Caribbean neighbours. Barbados is a member of the West Indian Common Market CARICOM and, in theory, should be able to have free access to these markets. However, recent downturns in the economies of these states, Trinidad and Tobago in particular, has meant the introduction of import duties. On the labour front, too, Barbados has its problems. While being able to offer the advantage of a relatively well educated and skilled labour force, it is often competing for factories that require low skills and low wages. The theoretical answer to this is that Barbados's industry must improve its productivity and encourage activities that can offer a high local added value — and the future of its manufacturing industry hinges on whether or not it can face these challenges.

Agriculture and fishing

In pre-independence days, agriculture was the corner-stone of the local economy. Today it is in rapid decline and all Barbadian political parties agree that something must be done to stem this drop in production. The collapse of the sector is particularly worrying if correlated to the dangers of overdependence on tourism and the ups-and-downs of manufacturing. Sugar, of course, is the main crop, but harvests have been declining in recent years and today sugar accounts for only 3.9 per cent of the GDP. West Indian sugar cannot compete on world markets due to high costs, and its survival depends on favourable export agreements to the EEC and the USA. There have been a number of reasons for the decline, from weather problems to poor management and the move from the countryside to the town. Nonetheless the industry does bring in US$35m a year and supports 6,000 jobs. Furthermore, sugar-cane plays a vital role in maintaining the island's thin layer of topsoil in place. Without the canes or other grasses to prevent erosion, Barbados would soon become a desert.

In recent years the Government has also encouraged diversification in agriculture, including cotton (now second only to sugar), cattle breeding and tropical fruit production. Barbados is in fact heavily dependent on food imports and could use some of its fallow land for food crops. However, strange as it may seem, the phenomenon of food imports is nothing new, as even in the seventeeth century planters preferred to import food rather than lose any of their land for sugar-cane production. Furthermore, it may be pointed out that if it were not for the imports of food from the poorer Caribbean states, such as St Vincent and St Lucia, these trading partners of Barbados would not have the wherewithall to buy Barbadian manufactured goods or services.

Fishing too can be considered with agriculture, and there are several fishing ports along the west coast, the most important being Bridgetown, Oistins and Speightstown. Demand, however, outstrips supply, especially in the tourist season; the fruits of overfishing are coming to roost. On the other hand, the fishing fleet and port facilities have been improved and today the boats are going further afield to find their catch. For example, in 1989 an agreement was signed between Barbados and Guyana which allows Bajan boats to fish in Guyanese waters.

Services

Finally, we can say that there are also some developments in a new sector — the service industry. Barbados, with its excellent communications networks, is now becoming a pole for regional financial services, including banking and insurance. It even has a Stock Market (opened in 1987), one of the smallest in the world, but nonetheless one which was able to avoid the tempest of Black Monday of the same year.

A martello tower at Heywoods (St Peter) is a reminder of the island's military history. Barbados was the leading British base in the West Indies and as such was open to French attack.

ELEVEN

Historical outline

Amerindian Barbados

Unlike many Caribbean islands, Barbados was not discovered by Christopher Columbus on one of his voyages to the New World, the reason for this probably being that Barbados lies well to the east of the chain of volcanic islands that makes up the Antilles. However, it would seem that the Spaniards who followed in Columbus's wake were to be the first Europeans to visit the island. They did not settle Barbados but sent raiding parties to carry off Carib Indians as slaves. This would have been after the Spanish Cedula of 1511 which decreed that 'cannibals' could be enslaved — and the very word 'Carib' derives from the Spanish word for cannibal. Whether all the Caribs were enslaved or whether others died of disease or emigrated is unknown, however, when the Portuguese captain Pedro a Campos called at the island in 1536 it was probably uninhabited.

The Caribs, in fact, were the last of the Amerindian peoples to settle Barbados, the others being the Barrancoids and the Arawaks. Evidence would sugggest that the **Barrancoids** originally inhabited the Orinoco basin and moved up through the Caribbean islands to Barbados at about the time of Christ and are thought to have remained for about six centuries. Remains of Barrancoid pottery have been found on various sites on the island and can be seen in the Barbados Museum. So far little is known about their civilisation, except that they were skilled potters.

The Barrancoids were followed in about 800 AD by the **Arawaks**. They too came originally from the Orinoco basin and moved northward to occupy the Lesser and Greater Antilles. What do we know about the Arawaks? From the reports of the early chroniclers the Arawaks were olive-skinned, of medium height, with flattened faces. They wore few or no clothes. It would seem that they were a kind and gentle people who preferred fishing to hunting. They made their large canoes by hollowing out a felled silk-cotton tree with hot coals, sometimes adding a sail. Certainly such craft were ill-suited to the Atlantic swell and in fact the Arawaks largely ignored the east coast of Barbados. They had agriculture too and grew cassava, maize, papayas, pineapples, peanuts and tobacco which they smoked or chewed, a habit they were to introduce to the Europeans. Another Arawak product which was 'exported' to Europe was the hammock, indeed the very word (along with 'hurricane', 'savannah' and 'canoe') is of Amerindian origin. They would have also been attracted to Barbados by the abundance of clay, the raw material for their highly attractive pottery — and Barbados still has a tradition for pottery as the visitors will discover for themselves should they call in at Chalky Mount. The Arawak village was headed by a chief who inherited power through his mother's family and lived in a large rectangular house, as against the round houses of his subjects. Another characteristic that differentiated the chief was the fact that only he could have more than one wife. Arawak villages were sited at such places as Pie Corner (St Lucy), Silver Sands (Christ Church) and Indian River (just north of Bridgetown). The Arawak civilisation on Barbados lasted about four centuries — why they disappeared from the island is a matter of speculation. Did they spontaneously decide to abandon the island or were they killed off or driven away by invading Caribs?

The **Caribs** (they called themselves Kalinago) too came from the Orinoco basin, moving from island to island up the 'Caribbean Way', arriving in Barbados around 1200 AD. They too were olive-skinned, with flat foreheads and noses and wore little or no clothing. They were a fierce and warlike people with a reputation for cannibalism — though some historians would argue that this aspect has been exaggerated by those who wished to enslave them because according to the Spanish Cedula of 1511 only cannibals could be enslaved. They excelled as sailors and fishermen but not as potters, for their pottery is not as refined as that produced by the Arawaks — indeed captured Arawak women were greatly appreciated for their skills in this field. Another important difference between the Arawaks and the Caribs is that while the former had heriditary leaders the Carib leaders were usually elected for their courage and skill.

From the quantity of Carib pottery found on Barbados it has been deduced that the island may well have been the Carib headquarters in the Caribbean. It was from here that the raiding parties of fierce warriors left to drive terror into the peaceful Arawaks. To make themselves look even more ferocious the warriors would gash their faces with agouti teeth and paint white circles round their eyes. The fate that met their enemies was certain death, whether in battle or later as prisoners, before being served up as a meal. Boys would be castrated and fattened up as a delicacy while captured women were kept as concubines.

The fate of the Caribs on Barbados is a matter of speculation but the two most acceptable theories are that they were carried off into slavery by Spanish raiding parties, or that they died of disease brought to the island by European sailors. What is certain is that when the first English settlers landed in 1627 there were no Amerindians living there, and some historians would claim that as early as 1536, when Pedro a Campos came to Barbados, the island was uninhabited.

The early settlers

The Spanish and the Portuguese
The early Spanish and Portuguese visitors never claimed Barbados for their respective thrones, nor did they leave traces of their short stays on the island, with one important exception — the island's name. The term Barbados — 'the bearded ones' — is said to owe its origin to the bearded fig trees with their aerial roots which so impressed the Portuguese sailors as to induce them to name the island after them.

Claimed in the name of James I
The first English ship to visit the island was the *Olive Blossom* on 14 May 1625, after having been blown off course on its voyage from Brazil to England. Captain John Powell landed some men at the present-day Holetown and claimed the island in the name of King James I of England. Powell returned to England and persuaded his employer, Sir William Courteen, to send an expedition back to establish a settlement. Two years later, on 17 February 1627, John Powell's brother, William, landed at Holetown (then called Jamestown) with some eighty English settlers and ten negro slaves (who had been captured from a Spanish ship) to start a colony that was to remain in English hands until independence in 1966.

Courteen and Carlisle

The early settlers found a wooded island but they soon set to work clearing the trees and, with the aid of some Amerindians brought in from Guyana, began to produce crops such as yams, plantains, cassava, maize, cotton and tobacco. More settlers followed, all of whom were in the pay of the merchant Courteen, but soon the ownership of the island was to be disputed between Courteen and the Earl of Carlisle. Both men sought royal grants and eventually, after much deceit and wrangling, Carlisle won. Courteen's men on Barbados resisted Carlisle's Governor for some time but were forced to surrender to Carlisle's second Governor, Henry Hawley, who proved to be highly unpopular. Carlisle's men began to settle further south, on the site of the present-day capital, Bridgetown, whose bay still bears the name Carlisle.

Indentured servants

The 1630s saw the arrival of a large influx of indentured servants from the British Isles who did most of the servile and agricultural work, while the number of negro slaves remained comparatively low (estimated at 6,000 in 1643 as against 37,000 whites). Some of these indentured servants were volunteers, ready to be bound to one master for a period of five to seven years, after which time they would be given a sum of money or a piece of land. Others had less choice — persons convicted of minor offences asked to be transported to the colonies rather than face the gallows, and as demand outstripped supply quite a number of men, women and children were kidnapped and put on ships bound for Barbados (the term 'to barbadoes' was coined for this operation), where they would have to serve a long period of bondage. Political opponents and prisoners of conscience became fair game for transportation to the colonies too. This 'tradition' was started by Oliver Cromwell after the Irish rebellion of 1649 and continued with the Jacobite risings in the eighteenth century.

These poor whites (whose descendents can still be found today in some of the East Coast parishes) or 'red legs', as they were known, toiled under the harshest of conditions and could be punished at the whim of their masters. It is not surprising that they tried to rebel, but insurrections were quickly put down and the rebels hanged.

On a more positive note, however, when their contracts expired they were given small plots of land and became those yeomen farmers who were to play quite a significant role in the island's history. In fact as early as 1645 they accounted for about a third of the island's white population.

The Public Buildings, Bridgetown, seat of the Barbadian Parliament. The island's House of Assembly dates from 1639 (not in the present building) giving it one of the oldest parliaments in the New World.

The House of Assembly

On the political front too, Barbados was making progress with the creation of its House of Assembly in 1639, on the instigation of Hawley, who was rebelling against dismissal by the second Earl of Carlisle. Hawley, the schemer and intriguer, decided to court popularity by establishing something which he knew most wealthy Barbadians wanted, autonomy and the chance to draw up their own laws. Hawley was eventually forced to quit, but the institution he founded was to continue to function through the centuries and was the forerunner of the present democratic Parliament.

Cavaliers and Roundheads

The English Civil War or English Revolution of the 1640s at first left Barbados relatively unscathed. Refugees of both sides came to the island and lived in relative peace. Both Cavaliers and Roundheads accepted not to mention 'Cavalier' or 'Roundhead' in company, and those who forgot this etiquette were bound by the so-called 'Treaty of Turkey and Roast Pork' to provide a turkey and a pig for a sumptuous meal for those who had heard the offending remark. However, by 1650 the climate had changed. The Cavalier refugees far outnumbered the Roundheads and began to challenge Cromwell, and Commonwealth England, by declaring allegiance to the exiled son of Charles I and commanding the use of the Common Prayer Book. The future king sent Lord Willoughby to the island as his representative and Governor, who did much to calm the waters and restore the peace between the warring factions. However, the English Parliament was deeply offended by Barbados's allegiance to Charles, and Cromwell decided to send a fleet to subdue the rebellious colony. Willoughby and the Barbadians decided to resist the 'imperialist' invasion and mustered an army of over six thousand men. The commander of the English fleet knew his forces were not sufficient to take the island by storm and tried different tactics to bring the Barbadians to heel, including an embargo on shipping, but his master stroke was persuading a group of moderate Royalists under Colonel Modiford to join forces with him; Willoughby sued for peace rather than face a bloody battle. The result was the 'Articles of Agreement' signed at the Mermaid Tavern in Oistins: the 'Articles' proved to be a sort of charter of autonomy for the island and strengthened the hand of the Assembly in its right to legislate for Barbadians.

From tobacco to sugar

In the early years as a colony, the Barbadian economy was based on cash crops such as cotton, ginger and in particular tobacco. However, the latter could not compete for quality with Virginian produce and, moreover, the English imposed a tax on Barbadian tobacco. Apparently the aim of this tax was to encourage Barbados to grow more food and to be less dependent on Dutch traders, but ironically it was the Dutch who stepped in to rescue the island's wheezing economy, by introducing sugar-cane and the technology to manufacture sugar. The crop that was to be known 'King Sugar' was brought to Barbados from Brazil by Pieter Blower in 1637 and in a few years was to revolutionise the island's economy and to make it dependent on the African slave trade.

Sugar, slavery and the plantation system

It was sugar that put the Caribbean islands on the map and that made 'tiny specks' in the ocean appetisable to the Great Powers of the seventeenth and eighteenth centuries. Islands such as St Lucia were to change hands as many as 14 times between England and France and stability came only with the defeat of Napoleonic France. Today it is difficult to appreciate the value that was attached to this everyday product, the demand for which rose rapidly as the European economies expanded in the eighteenth century. In a letter published in *The Economist* in 1988, a reader wrote of the calculation (using gold as the standard of comparison) of the price of sugar in the eighteenth century in modern terms — 'the price of sugar in the eighteenth century was about $5,500 per tonne as against $160 in 1985'. And when we consider that the planter used slave labour it is easy to imagine the profits made.

Mass emigration

Sugar-cane production was to transform radically the pattern of agriculture and the ethnic balance of the island. There was a sharp decline in the number of smallholdings and mass emigration of Barbadian whites in the period 1650-1680. The 1684 census showed a white population of less than 20,000 compared with about 40,000 in the 1630s. These white emigrants consisted mainly of freed indentured servants who had little or no land to cultivate and the smallholder or peasant farmer who saw no future for themselves in a society that was dominated by a few hundred large estates. Sugar production, in fact, demanded considerable investment in land, machinery and labour which only the wealthy could afford and as the supply of indentured white labourers dried up (many had been attracted by the idea of a smallholding after their period of indenture) the planters turned increasingly to importing slaves from West Africa.

African slaves

Originally it was the Dutch who supplied the island with slaves but the English Parliament disapproved of foreign ships supplying the colony and soon the Royal Africa Company was established with the aim of supplying England's West Indian islands with their labour force for the plantations. Slaving increased throughout the eighteenth century and it is estimated that in one decade alone, from 1791 to 1801, the British Caribbean imported over 1,400,000 slaves, of which 250,000 went to Barbados. The death rate, both at sea and on the plantation, was enormous, with overseers proudly reporting that they had been able to increase production at the cost of slaves' lives.

Slavery changed the pattern of life in Barbados. The whites were soon outnumbered by their slaves and the Assembly, which was by now totally in the hands of the plantocracy, passed repressive laws to thwart the danger of slave revolts. These indeed did occur and were ruthlessly put down, but they were relatively infrequent compared to those on other islands. The reason for this was that Barbados offered no forest refuge for runaway slaves and that failure meant certain death. Some historians would also claim that a high percentage of slaves were born on the island and were more passive than recently imported slaves, although the above figures concerning the importing of slaves would seem to contradict this affirmation.

Breadfruit — slave fodder

The slaves' living conditions were abysmal, with long working hours in the field and miserable food and clothing supplies. Their typical weekly food rations would be: 28 lbs of ground provisions (yam or potatoes), 10 pints of corn, half a pound of saltfish and some molasses. The breadfruit tree was introduced to the Caribbean by Captain Bligh (of *Mutiny on the Bounty* fame) as an alternative to ground provisions. It supplied bountiful supplies of carbohydrates but required little care, and the precious land which would otherwise have been taken up with provisions could be used in sugar production.

Slave society

In their free time slaves liked to meet for dances and singing and the night represented the most joyous moment of the slave's life. White society however despised and feared these musical encounters and a law was passed to forbid the playing of drums and other noisy instruments. Another characteristic of Barbados was the influence of the Anglican Church — or maybe the influence which the planters had on the Anglican Church — which became one of the strongholds of the gulf between white and black society. Unlike what happened on Catholic Caribbean islands, slaves were not allowed to become Christians and whites managed to preserve a mystique around their religion which the slaves interpreted as a sort of magical ceremony.

Just as white Barbadians had their hierarchy with the planters at the top, followed by the manager and the overseer, clerks and tradesmen, with poor white smallholders at the bottom of the pyramid, slave society too had its social divisions. Slaves' status would be judged not only from their job, field slaves enjoying least prestige while drivers, skilled craftsmen and domestic slaves were higher in the social scale, but also the personal position of their master could enhance their standing in slave society. One of the major criticisms of modern Barbadian society is that it is 'class-ridden', and there would certainly seem to be deep-rooted historical grounds for this affirmation.

Free coloureds

However, eighteenth-century Barbadian society cannot be neatly divided into two categories, a free white minority and an enslaved black majority. Unions between the two ethnic groups gave birth to mulattos or 'coloureds' and often the white masters would sign the manumission papers for the child, and sometimes for the slave mother. The numbers of free coloured people was further swelled by masters and mistresses who decided to free their slaves after many years of faithful service. Since this was open to abuse, in that manumission could be used as a cynical way of getting rid of old and infirm slaves who could not provide for their own upkeep, a law passed in 1739 obliged owners to pay a fee on manumission. In theory this may have been enlightened and humane but in practice it simply put a brake on the growing free black population that was viewed with concern in many circles. In fact many free coloureds became quite successful in business and farming, even to become slave-owning planters by the end of the century.

The last slave rebellion

In the meantime liberal opinion in Britain was coalescing towards the abolition of slavery in the British Empire — slavery had already been abolished in 1794 in France as one of the libertarian measures of the Revolution, but was to be re-introduced a few years later by Napoleon. The first success of the reformers was the abolition of slave trading (1807) which proved only partially successful. To enforce the law the reformers proposed the introduction of the registration of existing slaves, but Barbadian planters strongly objected to this on the grounds that it was a matter for the Barbadian Assembly. This led to the last slave rebellion in Barbadian history in 1816. Ironically this was brought about by a misunderstanding of the controversy which the slaves had heard about. They had thought that it was not a question of registration, but of the abolition of slavery, and that the planters were trying to thwart this. The leaders were some free coloured men and a slave called Bussa, and on Good Friday of 1816 they met to make final arrangements for the insurrection which was to start on the night of Easter Sunday. Cane fields in St George were set on fire and soon the fires spread to other southern parishes. Naturally the unarmed slaves were no match for the army and the militia and were soon defeated — about 176 slaves died in battle as against one white militiaman and over 200 were later executed for their part in the revolt.

Emancipation

The abolition of slavery
However, the planters' victory was shortlived for pressure was constantly mounting in Britain for the complete abolition of slavery — the reformers were no longer a handful of influential liberals, but now enjoyed the backing of the churches, including, finally, the Anglican Church. On 28 August 1833 the Westminster Parliament finally passed the Act that abolished slavery (from 1 August 1834) throughout the British Empire. However, to avoid the breakdown of 'law and order', the so-called apprenticeship system was introduced. The idea was to tie the ex-slave to a certain job for a certain number of years to guarantee the plantation owner a sure supply of labour and, at the same time, to 'train' the ex-slaves for their freedom. This apprenticeship lasted until 1 August 1838 when Emancipation throughout the British West Indies was achieved. The event was marked in Barbados by the joyous celebrations by the black population — in the words of one famous folk song of the period:

> Lick an' lock-up done wid,
> Hurrah fuh Jin-Jin!

The young Queen Victoria (Jin-Jin) became their hero as emancipation meant an end to jailings (lock-up) and floggings (lick) — indeed a milestone in Bajan history.

Maintaining the status quo
The coming of emancipation raised great expectations in the minds of the black population, while the planters feared losing their cheap labour force as some blacks began to emigrate to other islands

where pay was better. To counter this potential trend in 1840 the planters introduced legislation — known as the Masters and Servants Act — that was to have a lasting effect on Barbados for over a century. This ensured a sort of feudal system whereby labourers guaranteed their services at less than market rate in return for a minimum of security. In fact the dice were loaded heavily in favour of the planters who by this means were able to guarantee themselves a supply of labour at less than half the price of some of their neighbours. One of the reasons for the 'success' of this system was that, unlike in neighbouring territories, in Barbados there was no free land where blacks could set up villages and start smallholdings. With the notable exceptions of a few liberals such as Samuel Jackman Prescod (a mulatto who managed to get himself elected to the House of Assembly), opinion that counted was all in favour of maintaining the status quo.

The years of crises

Crown Colony controversy

In the 1870s the British Government began to consider making Barbados part of a Confederal Crown Colony with the Windward Islands and were supported in this plan by the Governor, John Pope Hennessey. Hennessy thought that this was the only was of breaking the hold of the plantocracy who controlled the House of Assembly and furthering the lot of the oppressed blacks. The House of Assembly's demand that the island's autonomy be respected led to rioting by blacks in favour of the Confederacy plan. Once again the planters won and Hennessy was transferred to Hong Kong.

Panama Money

The only way left open to blacks to bettering their lot was emigration. Between 1850 and 1914 thousands left for British Guyana, Trinidad and especially Panama. Some 20,000 men left the island to work as labourers building the canal. Many were able to save or to send money home to their families. 'Panama Money', linked to the falling price of land, meant that many blacks were able to buy land and set up as farmers in free villages. It also meant that many more blacks were able to get a decent education and swell the growing middle classes and urban dwellers.

Labour and social unrest

Emigration began to slow down after 1914 with the completion of the canal and the anti-immigrant policies of many traditional outlets. This only heightened the great economic crisis and social tension in Barbados between the two worlz wars. Bajan workers became increasingly aware politically and unionised under the influence of such organisations as Charles Duncan O'Neale's Democratic League, and later the Barbados Labour Party and the Barbados Workers' Union. Racial tensgon also increased due to the influence of black radicals such as Jamaican Marcus Garvey, who advocated a return to Africa. The situation came to a head in 1937 with riots throughout the West Indies, and the Barbados riots in particular were celebrated in a folk song called called the *Riot Song:*

> Listen friends to what was composed
> De twenty-seventh of July I couldn't show muh nose;
> Civilian wid rocks, policemen wid guns,
> Doan doubt mv friends it wasn't no fun
> For everytime dat yuh hear a round
> Somebody dead and somebody wound.

Barbadian theatre is lively and witty — if you can understand the Bajan dialect.

Barbadian writer George Lamming too gives vivid descriptions of the rioting in his novel *In the Castle of My Skin*: here young Bob describes what he had seen in the city: 'Then the crowds multiplied and the weapons too, and he felt sick in the stomach. He followed the men through the alleys and towards the sea. There was blood in the streets, but he was giddy with the sight of the weapons and the men standing along the waterfront. Occasionally the police attacked, and the men retaliated with stones and bottles. Some leapt into the sea, and others climbed the trees. The police were continually repulsed, and when the situation was beyond control, the shooting started.'

The Moyne Commission investigated the disturbances and reported to the Westminster Parliament of the plight of working class blacks in the West Indies, advocating reform. The Commission heard the evidence of some of the island's future leaders, men such as Grantley Adams and H.W. Springer representing the Progressive League.

Post-war developments

Universal suffrage

A number of measures were introduced to improve the economic lot of workers and, under great pressure from the Barbados Labour Party, political reform was introduced by the Governor after World War II. Despite diehard opposition from the white planters who controlled the Legislature, universal suffrage was introduced to the island in the 1951 general elections which resulted in a great victory for the Barbados Labour Party. The 1950s were marked by the establishment of a ministerial form of government, a split in the Labour Party which led to the formation of the Democratic Labour Party, and, in 1958, to the trouble-fraught experiment of the Federation of the West Indies, with Grantley Adams as Federal Prime Minister.

Federation

The idea of the Federation had been mooted in the early 1930s, the presupposition being that only by joining together could the West Indies obtain independence as a Dominion within the British Commonwealth. The aspiration towards independence was further stimulated after the war as countries such as India, Pakistan and Ceylon obtained this and it was clear that the rest of the British

Empire would eventually follow this road. The federalist spirit varied from island to island, with Trinidad and Grenada being the most enthusiastic supporters of a fully federal state while Jamaican and Barbadian leaders remained rather cooler towards the idea. However, the federation did come into being in 1958 but it lasted only four years owing to internal bickering between the two leading members, Jamaica and Trinidad and Tobago, with the smaller islands left with the feeling that they counted for very little.

Independence

In 1962 the Federation collapsed with the exit of Jamaica and Trinidad and Tobago, which became independent states within the Commonwealth in the same year. An attempt was made to set up a second federation of the remaining smaller islands of the Leeward and Windward Islands, plus Barbados, but after a good start to negotiations parochial jealousies got the better of the situation and talks collapsed. It was after this state of affairs that Barbadian leaders began to see that the only path left open to them was independence, which came to the island on 30 November 1966, after more than three centuries of British rule. A new nation was born as Prime Minister Errol Barrow (Democratic Labour Party) became the leader of what was to prove to be one of the most stable democracies in the region.

TWELVE

The people

Population

Barbados has about 260,000 people packed onto its 431 square kilometres (166 square miles) of territory, giving it one of the highest population densities in the western hemisphere. Population pressure has always been a problem on West Indian islands and the traditional solution has been emigration. Barbadians left the island in their thousands to build the Panama Canal, to toil in the Cuban sugar fields and to work in industry and services in North America and Britain. However, Barbadians, with one of the highest educational standards in the region, have also been at the forefront in supplying skilled workers and trained professionals and the island has been a traditional source of supply for policemen, nurses and teachers.

Strange as it may seem the visitor is often unaware of this population pressure, except in certain districts, for the population is not uniformly distributed. Bridgetown and the surrounding parish of St Michael alone have a population of 100,000 and there is a further concentration along the south and west coasts from Oistins to Speightstown. Besides Bridgetown, only Speightstown, Holetown and Oistins may be considered towns but most business is done in the capital.

Administratively the island is divided into parishes or districts which are, from north to south: St Lucy, St Peter, St Andrew, St Joseph, St James, St Thomas, St John, St George, St Michael, St Philip and Christ Church. Some of the northern and eastern parishes have a very sparse population and the atmosphere is very 'rural'.

About 90 per cent of the population is black, the descendents of the African slaves, 5 per cent is of mixed origin and less than 5 per cent is white. There are also small Asiatic communities. The white population consists of three main groups: the white 'aristocracy', descendents of the wealthy planters; the 'Red Legs' or poor whites, descendents of the indentured servants; recent white immigrants, often connected with the tourist industry or retired people. The whites still control much of the economy but political power is now in the hands of the black majority. Racial relations are generally harmonious, although in recent years some politicians have been voicing their concern at the concentration of economic power in the hands of the white minority.

In any case the visitor will find a sense of community and this can be best summed up with the expression 'All o' we is Bajan'. The Bajan dialect in fact is a unifying factor for it can be heard in all sections of the population. Perhaps it is this that unites black Bajans and the 'old' white population as distinct from the newcomers.

Another feature of Barbadian life is the 'family situation'. A very high proportion of Barbadians get married late in life or do not get married at all. 79 per cent of all children are born outside wedlock but this does not carry any social stigma and legitimate and illegitimate children have equal rights. They are brought up in an extended family environment by aunts, sisters and grandparents. The father is legally responsible for their upkeep, although this is often more in theory than in practice.

Religion

Anglicans

Religions and religious sects abound in Barbados, there being no fewer than 100 denominations and sects. The predominant group, however, is Anglican. At one time Barbados had one of the highest concentrations of Anglicans in the world (over 80 per cent of the population declared to be Anglican in the late 1880s); during this century there has been a decline to 53 per cent in 1970 (or even 31.7 per cent according to Graham Dann's survey in 1981), as increasing numbers of Anglicans were attracted to American-style sects. The Anglican Church has always been the church for the upper classes and for centuries reflected the planters' views to the exclusion of slaves from baptism. Many would still consider the Anglican religion 'a must' for those who consider social mobility important.

Methodists, Moravians and Catholics

The Methodist and Moravian Churches have also had an important historical role on the island for it was ministers of these denominations who fought for the rights of slaves in the eighteenth century, often at great personal expense against the wrath of the whites. According to the 1970 census, 8.6 per cent of the population were Methodists while 2.2 per cent were Moravians. As with other traditional religions these figures were redimensioned in Dann's survey which highlighted the success of certain sects and the fact that almost 40 per cent of those interviewed did not declare any religious affiliation. Another traditional church, the Roman Catholic, accounts for about 3 per cent of the population.

Rastafarianism

A phenomenon common to many West Indian islands has been the rise of Rastafarianism. The movement began in the 1920s when Jamaican-born Marcus Garvey founded his 'back to Africa' movement. He urged his followers to take a pride in their black heritage and promised the day of deliverance would be at hand when a black king was crowned in Africa. This prophecy was associated with the crowning of Ras Tafari as Emperor Haile Selassie in 1930, and Garvey's followers took on the name Rastafarians. The true Rasta lives a pious life, rejecting white man's consumer society, but frequently this image of the peaceful Rastafarian has been tarnished by events. The movement received a strong impulse in the 1970s from the Black Power movement in America and marijuana consumers often found Rastafarianism a convenient excuse. For some time the dread-locked movement was a magnet for rebellious youth and petty criminals and there was an upsurge in membership in Barbados in the late 1970s. For most it was a passing fad and numbers declined rapidly in the 1980s as the police clamped down on the more unruly elements and youth turned its attention to other interests. Today you will find the remaining Rastafarians mainly engaged in selling coconuts and in making leather and wooden objects (sold at the 'Rasta Mall' in Temple Yard, Bridgetown).

Government and politics

Barbados makes much of its long tradition of political stability and certainly it has enjoyed one of the most democratic and stable forms of government in the region since independence in 1966. Some would attribute this to the fact that the island has had a parliament since 1639, whilst others would prefer to play down this point a little, pointing out that a local assembly controlled by the plantocracy and firmly opposed to the abolition of slavery can hardly be considered the mother of democracy. However, the same criticism could also be levelled at other parliaments, including Westminster, before the nineteenth century reforms.

The system of government

Barbados is a constitutional monarchy, with Queen Elizabeth II as Head of State. The Queen is represented locally by the Governor General, who is appointed on the advice of the Prime Minister. The Governor General's powers include apppointing the Prime Minister and a minority of Senators. He also appoints the Privy Council which has important control functions over the Civil Service Commission and considers petitions from prisoners.

The Barbados Parliament has two chambers, the House of Assembly and the Senate. The House of Assembly consists of twenty-seven elected members representing the nation's twenty-seven constituencies. Elections follow the British pattern, using the 'first-past-the-post' system and not proportional representation, and are held at intervals of not more than five years. On the other hand, the Senate performs a similar role to the House of Lords, i.e. as a place where 'second opinions' are aired. Senators can delay legislation but not prevent it, as the majority of the 21 Senators can be dismissed by the Prime Minister, others being nominated by the Governor General and on the advice of the leader of the Opposition. The function and powers of Government are vested in the Cabinet, presided over by the Prime Minister.

Political parties

Barbados has had numerous parties during its 350 years of Parliamentary history, from the Pumpkins of the nineteenth century to the West Indian National Congress Party in the 1940s, and to the two parties that have dominated the scene since independence, the Barbados Labour Party and the Democratic Labour Party. The Westminister-style electoral system favours large parties and two-party systems. At the time of writing (1989), there are actually three parties in the Barbadian House of Assembly after a split in the Democratic Labour Party in 1988. The new party, called the New Democratic Party, however, has yet to face the ordeal of elections and it is too early to tell whether Barbados electors will confirm a three-party system or prefer to revert to two parties only.

Party loyalties are strong, with analysts calculating that only about 20 per cent of the electorate are open to persuasion. Politicians therefore tend to concentrate on trying to sway the middle ground voters and both traditional parties could be considered centre parties, with mild social democratic tendencies in the field of social reforms (especially health and education), and market-oriented economic policies. The outside observer, indeed, would probably have great difficulty in distinguishing between the two (which have a common heritage), and elections are won or lost on local issues or personalities.

From pre-independence days till 1985, Barbadian politics were dominated by two giants, Tom Adams and Errol Barrow, leaders of the Barbados Labour Party and the Democratic Labour Party respectively. For 25 years the island was led by a sort of Caribbean Gladstone-Disraeli duo and then, within the space of two years, both men died in office, Adams in 1985 and Barrow in 1987. Their successors are Mr Henry Forde, leader of the Barbados Labour Party and the present Prime Minister, Mr Erskine Sandiford, of the Democratic Labour Party. The New Democratic Party is led by Dr Richard Haynes, former Democratic Labour Party Finance Minister, and is trying to win the heart of the younger, more affluent urban and suburban voter.

A good track record

The two parties which have ruled the country since independence have both fostered the island's economy by promoting development in three sectors: tourism, manufacturing and agriculture. Although the economies of small nations inevitably depend almost entirely on external factors, making them extremely vulnerable in times of crisis, it must be recognised that Barbados has done better than most. It has seen a fair but steady increase in its Gross Domestic Product (an average of 2.6 per cent over seven years), giving it one of the highest standards of living in the Caribbean (1988 per capita income US$5,795) and progress has also been seen in many fields, including education and health.

A new protector and model

In international relations there have been major changes in the Caribbean in the last twenty years, with the loss of influence of the ex-colonial powers and the entry of the United States as the regional gendarme. Historically the importance of American influence in the region goes back much further, essentially to the days of World War II when Churchill leased bases in the British West Indies to the US Armed Forces. After the war American cultural influence grew steadily and now enters many homes directly through satellite TV. Politically too, Britain began to take less interest in the islands and concentrate its attention on Europe — the all-telling example of this came in 1983 with the US-led invasion of Grenada.

The late 1970s and early 1980s were a period of turmoil and political experimentation in many Caribbean islands and, at first, quite a few Caribbean politicians did not look unfavourably upon Maurice Bishop's left-wing government in Grenada. By 1983, however, the situation in Grenada was turning sour as the island became a pawn in the regional power struggle between the USA and Cuba. Bishop and several of his close advisors were assassinated by an ultra-Leninist clique within the regime, who then seized power. This was the situation that led up to the US-led invasion of Grenada shortly later. Barbados Prime Minister Tom Adams, in particular, was in favour of this 'rescue operation' (and the operation is genuinely considered such by the vast majority of West Indians), and it was one more example of what became known as the 'Adams Doctrine'. Adams was concerned that the small West Indian democracies could easily be subverted by a small internal minority with the support of an external power, and, as most of the islands did not have an army, he proposed a mobile inter-island force to deal with such threats. The 'Adams' Doctrine' was first applied in 1979 when St Vincent asked Barbados for military assistance in evicting an invasion force of alleged Rastafarians from Union Island. However, as Adams himself was to state in December 1983, 1983 was the 'watershed' year in which the influence of the United States, willy-nilly, came observably to replace that of Great Britain.

Education and social welfare

Education
Barbados with its 97 per cent literacy rate has one of the highest educational standards in the Caribbean. Barbadians have always attached great importance to education as a means of making social progress and the island has a long tradition of schools of good repute. The most famous secondary schools include Harrison's College, Lodge School, Queen's and Alexandra School. Originally

the schools were founded for whites only and it was not until 1818 that coloured children were admitted. Schooling is compulsory from the age of five to sixteen and free at all levels. Entrance to the secondary grammar schools depends on selection at the age of eleven.

At the end of this impressive palm-lined avenue lies Codrington College — a theological school founded in the 18th century.

The island also offers higher and further education facilities, including the Cave Hill campus of the University of the West Indies which provides degree courses in Arts, the Natural Sciences and Law. Codrington College, a theological college in St John, is also part of the University. To cater for the training of staff for the all-important tourist industry there is the Barbados Hotel School which accepts local and foreign students. Other institutions include the Samuel Jackman Prescod Polytechnic and a Teacher Training College.

The Government is trying to create new job opportunities for its educated work force by encouraging industries such as data processing and financial services.

Social services
Despite obviously limited budgets, over the the last thirty years successive Barbadian Governments have managed to set up a welfare state and social services which are the envy of some of its Caribbean neighbours. The buses may be crowded but they offer a reasonably good service; a National Health System is being developed with free hospital care at the modern Queen Elizabeth Hospital and health clinics dotted round the island; there are unemployment benefits and pensions (albeit low). The island also boasts a public library service which includes the Carnegie Library on Coleridge Street in Bridgetown and seven branches in the various parishes as well as a mobile library service. Visitors can borrow books at all branches against a returnable deposit.

Cultural tradition

Barbados's cultural traditions derive from the island's ethnic heritage. For centuries the only acceptable culture was one based on English upper- and middle-class standards of taste and anything connected with African culture was strictly taboo.
 The African slaves brought with them their love of music and dance and despite various legal and social prohibitions this culture has managed to survive. As early as the seventeenth century a law was passed prohibiting the beating of drums or the sounding of loud instruments, so much did Europeans fear them. The result was that African music was driven underground and reserved for the secret gatherings of slaves at night. Among the music the slaves brought with them was a forerunner of the modern calypso, a musical vehicle for carrying news with a strong pinch of irony and social criticism.

Tuk band and the 'Landship'
For over a century after emancipation the British influence was so strong that anything connected with Africa remained socially unacceptable and the wandering minstrels would be considered as lepers. African music was called 'monkey music'. This ostracism led to two curious developments, the 'tuk band' and the 'Landship'. The former consists of a small band using British military instruments (bass drum, kettle drum and fife) to produce very non-British rhythms. The tuk bands toured (and still tour) the villages inviting the inhabitants to join in the fun and improvise dances. You will sometimes find a tuk band playing at a wedding. The Landship

Movement began in the last century as a sort of self-help organisation for ex-sailors who missed the camaraderie of the life at sea. The Movement became a curious mixture of a co-operative with savings and loans facilities, a character-building association for young people and entertainers all rolled into one. At the same time it gave Barbadians an opportunity to subtly make fun of British pomp. Each group is organised as a 'ship' with officers and ratings and adopts a well-starched naval-style uniform. The ship's company 'marches' to the accompaniment of a tuk band and guarantees an entertaining performance as they break into a pompous limbo.

Calypso and steel bands

Over recent years, especially since independence, most Caribbean islands have been heavily influenced by Trinidadian developments in the field of music. Steel bands and the tremendous popularity of calypso music have spread from island to island. Ironically it was a white Bajan group — The Merrymen — that led to a revival of calypso in Barbados in the 1960s. They were followed by a new generation of calypsonians such as Mighty Gabby and The Red Plastic Bag. Calypso became an important form of social and political criticism and occasionally certain songs were banned from the airwaves. Calypso can be heard all year round in Barbados but things build up to a peak in late July when there are the calypso competitions for Crop Over celebrations. The title of Calypso Monarch is worth much in prestige and commercial success.

Theatre

Barbadian theatre too has made great progress since independence. Popular folk comedy can be sampled at the Queen's Park Theatre while theatre workshops tour the villages offering a mix of farce and dance. Visitors, however, are more likely to be attracted or shepherded to the excellent dinner shows the island offers. These offer a sophisticated insight into Afro-Caribbean culture to the accompaniment of a sumptuous dinner (more details are given in Chapter 8).

Independence Day (30 November) is celebrated with The National Independence Festival of the Creative Arts. During the month, Barbadians of all ages compete in the fields of music, singing, dancing, acting and writing, then on 30 November there are the finals as well as photographic and arts and crafts exhibitions.

Nelson's statue in Trafalgar Square — the heart of Bridgetown. The continued presence of this statue is a matter of some controversy.

THIRTEEN

Bridgetown and St Michael

Bridgetown is the bustling heart of the nation and is sited at the northern end of Carlisle Bay. Today the town and its immediate suburbs accommodate about 100,000 of the 260,000 islanders. All roads lead to the capital and nothing could be more true for Bridgetown, which is the lopsided hub of the Barbados road network. This is reflected in the bus service too, with bus stops marked 'to city' and 'out of city'. For many visitors the heat and the traffic make Bridgetown suitable for a quick shopping trip and little else, which is a pity for the city does offer places of interest. For those who wish to avoid the crowds and traffic I suggest a Sunday visit when the city centre is almost deserted.

History

Bridgetown is the second oldest settlement on the island, being founded in 1628, shortly after Holetown. It was settled by pioneers sent out to the island by the Earl of Carlisle who had laid claim to Barbados. The original settlement was known simply as the Bridge, and was situated around the creek that was later to become the Careenage. The surrounding land was swampy but soon it became clear that Bridgetown was the most suitable site as the main settlement because of its central position to the outlying estates and because it did provide the best harbour, with the Careenage offering sheltered berthing for repairing ships. In 1656 a small fort, Willoughby's Fort was built at the seaward edge of the Careenage to defend the expanding town from external threat. The main commercial area of the original settlement seems to correspond to the present commercial hub of the city, centred on Broad Street (then known as Cheapside) and Swan Street. Unfortunately many of the historical buildings have been destroyed by fire, hurricanes, old age or simply property development, but enough remain to give Bridgetown some old charm alongside the concrete and glass of the ultra-modern offices and banks.

What to see

Trafalgar Square

If you wish to fix a meeting point in Bridgetown the place that most readily comes to mind is under **Nelson's statue** in **Trafalgar Square,** admittedly not the most suitable of places in the burning tropical sun, but Trafalgar Square is to Bridgetown what Piccadilly Circus is to London. The Square itself was originally known as the Green. Nelson had visited Barbados in 1805, not long before the Battle of Trafalgar, and Barbadians were somewhat quicker than Londoners in dedicating a square and erecting a statue to their hero. The bronze statue by Sir Richard Westmacott dates from 1813 and has ever since been the butt of considerable controversy, especially since independence.

The old port

To the south the Square overlooks the picturesque **Careenage** which is crossed by two bridges — the narrow Chamberlain Bridge (once a swing bridge) which leads directly into Trafalgar Square and, more to the east, the modern Charles Duncan O'Neal Bridge, named after one of the founders of the Barbadian trade union movement. Until 1961 the Careenage was the island's main port facility, larger ships having to anchor in the bay for loading and unloading, and was once bustling with inter-island schooner traffic. Today it is mainly the marina for pleasure craft as commercial traffic is now catered for in the modern Deep Water Harbour to the north of the city. The Careenage is lined by some interesting warehouse buildings and at the south end of the Chamberlain Bridge one of these buildings today houses a fashionable café and restaurant — a nice port of call for lunch or a refreshing drink, with a fine view of the port and the town. Chamberlain Bridge itself was embellished with an arch in 1988 to commemorate the 21st anniversary of independence.

Opposite: *Kadooment Day (the 1st Monday in August) marks the end of the Cropover Festival. All Barbados seems to take to the streets for the carnival-style road march.*

A parliamentary tradition

The **Public Buildings,** which at first sight many a visitor takes for the cathedral, housing the island's Parliament or House of Assembly, are located on the north side of Trafalgar Square. This Victorian complex was completed in 1874 and is only the latest of a long list of locations where Barbados's parliament has met, including private homes and taverns. In fact the island's Parliament has more than 350 years of history, having assembled for the first time in 1639. As a reminder of the long association with Britain you will note that the English monarchs from James I to Victoria are represented in the building's stained-glass windows.

The spiritual overshadowed by the temporal

Continuing in a north-easterly direction we come to St Michael's Row and the nation's most important church — **St Michael's Anglican Cathedral.** This has the dignified but unimposing air of what would be the parish church in a small English town. The original St Michael's Church was a wooden building on the site of the present St Mary's Church at Cheapside, but it was moved to the present location in 1665. The present building dates back to 1789, the previous one being destroyed in a hurricane in 1780. It became a cathedral in 1825 when William Hurst Coleridge was consecrated as Bishop. Coleridge is remembered as the Anglican who recognised the rights of slaves to practise the Anglican religion — previously the Anglicans had conveniently supported the planter theory that the slaves were little more than beasts and as such could not be baptised as Christians. By the end of the last century well over 80 per cent of the population were Anglicans — today the number is down to about 53 per cent (or even less according to some surveys), but it is still the predominant denomination.

The modern skyscraper that dominates Bridgetown's skyline and looms over the cathedral is the **Central Bank** building — many consider it to be out of all proportion to the city's dimension and a bit of a white elephant, others would consider it as a symbol of a new nation with a dynamic economy that is moving away from sugar cane estates into the world of high technology communications and services.

Opposite: *Cobblers Cove Hotel near Speightstown — one of the smaller but more luxurious properties.*

Central Bridgetown

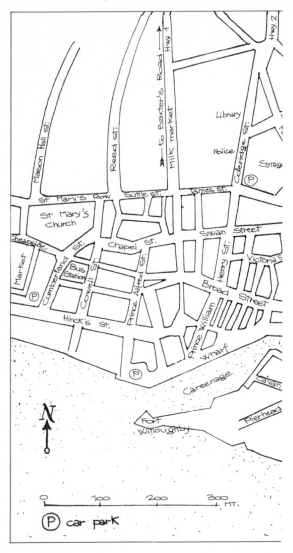

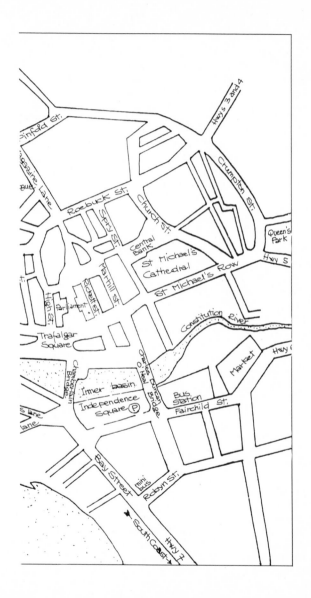

City greenery

By now you may wish to rest for a while and one of the most pleasant places to do so lies only a few minutes' walk from the cathedral — **Queen's Park.** Just keep going along St Michael's Row and you will find the entrance on the left.

The park was once the gardens of the British Commanding General's residence known as **Queen's House.** The house has been beautifully restored and is now used as a theatre and exhibition rooms. Opposite the house are some cages containing green Barbadian monkeys. However, if you wish to photograph monkeys, I recommend going to the Wildlife Reserve instead where you can find them in almost natural surroundings. Just past the house, on your left, you will see an enormous baobab tree (16.5 metres in girth). Barbadians make something of a mystery of this tree — the baobab is of African origin and this fine specimen is estimated to be over a thousand years old, thus predating by far Columbus's discovery of the New World!

The commercial centre and an old community

Let us now make our way back to Trafalgar Square and the city centre. West of the square lies Bridgetown's main shopping street — **Broad Street.** Here you will find a good assortment of banks, department stores and boutiques catering for the foreign visitor and the island's expanding middle classes. Some of the department stores have branches round the island but the Broad Street shops have a better selection of goods. Turning up Prince William Henry Street, we reach **Swan Street,** another shopping street but the tone is more for 'ordinary folks'. At one time this street was once known as Jews Street, owing to the fact that there was once a thriving Jewish community here. It was in fact Dutch Jews who introduced sugar cane to the island in the seventeenth century. A synagogue and Jewish cemeteries once existed in this area but fell into disuse when the Jewish community emigrated to America in the nineteenth century. Attempts are being made today to restore the synagogue and part of the cemetery which are located in Magazine Lane.

The overflow church

If we proceed down Broad Street and its continuation, Lower Broad Street, on the left we find the bus terminus (for buses to the west coast and north) and a narrow street known as **Temple Yard.** Temple Yard is a sort of workshop-cum-market for Rastafarian craftsmen offering interesting wood and leather works. On the right we come to **St Mary's Church** which stands on the original site of

St Michael's Cathedral. St Mary's was built in 1827 to accommodate the overflow of worshippers from St Michael's.

Markets

Those who are self-catering often notice the lack of greengrocers in their local shopping facilities and this can be particularly disappointing if you had been waiting to savour some of those exotic fruits and vegetables you have read about. The fact is that Bajans either 'grow their own' or they shop at one of the two main markets in town. Both are near important bus stations, **Fairchild Street** on the south side of Charles Duncan O'Neale Bridge and **Cheapside**, almost opposite St Mary's Church. Here you will find everything from 'English' potatoes to eddoes and yams, from plantains to soursop and custard apples. If you are not sure how to cook the vegetables just ask the 'hucksters', as the market sellers are known.

If you are looking for handicrafts and works of art you may well be interested in visiting **Pelican Village,** where a wide assortment of stalls and boutiques are located in attractive premises. As the village was built primarily with cruise passengers in mind, it is located along the Princess Alice Highway, near the Deep Water Harbour, about half an hour's walk from the city centre.

Bridgetown by night

Most visitors will probably confine their night life to the resort areas along the south and west coasts, perhaps in the vicinity of their hotels. It should be remembered that, unlike European capitals, Bridgetown itself does not offer any tourist accommodation, apart from a few minor guest houses, and people do not come here for the bright lights. Two streets, however, do seem to offer a little more life to night owls. One is **Bay Street** which is on the south side of Chamberlain Bridge, and is in fact the first part of the South Coast Road. Together with Nelson Street (almost parallel to it), it forms the city's red light district. One of the more reputable establishments is the Belair Jazz Club where you can meet an interesting cross-section of Bajan society.

Looking for a snack and a drink in the small hours? If you are not too fussy about fancy decor, then try **Baxter's Road,** the street with the reputation that 'it never sleeps'. Here you will find delicious fried flying fish, straight from the pan, or barbecued chicken at prices for the locals. Baxter's Road is not in the centre itself but in a rather rundown area north of Broad Street — turn right into Milkmarket Street which eventually leads into Baxter's Road.

Places of interest near Bridgetown

Military history buffs will find plenty to interest them in the
Garrison Savannah area, a couple of kilometres south of the city
centre. And even for those just interested in the history of the
island, a visit to this area is a must.

If you are driving, just follow the main road south (Bay Street)
out of the city and look for the turning on the left marked the
Barbados Museum (near the Light and Power Building). If you are
using public transport then take one of the south coast buses from
Fairchild bus terminus and ask to be put off at the Savannah.

The Garrison Savannah
This large open area was once the parade ground for the British
troops stationed on the island, but today it is one of the island's
most important sports venues, used for horse racing, soccer, rugby,
or simply jogging. There are several fine buildings that surround the
Savannah, one of the most characteristic being the **Savannah Club,**
with its distinctive cupola perched on top of the clock tower. The
building dates from the early years of the nineteenth century and
was originally the guard-house.

The Barbados Museum
At the north end of the Savannah we find the Barbados Museum,
which is housed in what was once the 'glass house' or military
prison and dates from about 1820. As it is laid out today it certainly
does not convey the air of misery that the prisoners must have
suffered here — nevertheless, the exhibition rooms are the ex-cells
(some with the original doors) and the pleasant courtyard that
makes such an attractive setting for the dinner show '1627 and all
that' was once the exercise yard. Today the museum (open Monday-
Saturday 9.00 am to 6.00 pm — small entrance fee) is the result of
over 50 years of hard work by the members of the Barbados
Museum and Historical Society and offers the visitor a fine
collection of Amerindian artefacts, interesting maps and prints
relating to the island's history, plantation house furniture, china,
silver and glassware, as well as a section on natural history. Guests
at the dinner show are encouraged to wander around the museum
before their evening's entertainment — a portrayal of history
through the slave's eyes.

The forts

Returning to the main coast road we pass other attractive nineteenth-century buildings on the east side of the Savannah all of which were part of the military establishment. On the seaward side of the coast road we find **St Anne's Fort.** The fort was started in 1704 but was never completed to the original ambitious plan. The early eighteenth-century ramparts, however, can still be seen. The fort was part of the island's fortifications against threat of French attack, especially during the American War of Independence. Today the fort is the headquarters of the Barbados Defence Force.

By taking the street called Aquatic Gap, just north of St Anne's Fort we come to **Needham's Point,** with its lighthouse and the Barbados Hilton Hotel. In the grounds of this hotel we find the remains of what was **Fort Charles,** with its battery of cannons which once defended the entrance to Carlisle Bay.

Hot and tired after your tour? Then why not take a dip and cool off at Needham's Point which offers one of the most attractive beaches on the island?

Government House and Belleville

The road round the Savannah, past the Barbados Museum, is a sort of inner ring road and if we continue along this, after the first roundabout we enter the elegant suburb of **Belleville,** consisting of ten well-planned avenues with many nineteenth-century wooden houses, including the Head Office of the Barbados National Trust **(Ronald Tree House,** 10th Avenue) and **Erdiston** which once belonged to the designer of the suburb, Sam Manning, and to Sir Graham Briggs, who was once also owner of the most sumptuous house on the island — Farley Hill. Erdiston now houses a college of education. At the north end of the neighbourhood, near the second roundabout, we find **Government House,** the official residence of the Queen's Representative in Barbados, the Governor General. The house has been in government hands since the early eighteenth century and is a fine example of a Barbadian Great House, with jalousied windows, verandahs and beautiful gardens. The house is not generally open to the public. Not far away, at Two Mile Hill, is the official residence of the Prime Minister, **Ilaro Court.** This neo-classical style coralstone residence was designed by Lady Gilbert Carter in 1919. Her husband, Sir Gilbert Carter, was Governor of the island at the beginning of the century.

West Coast and St Michael

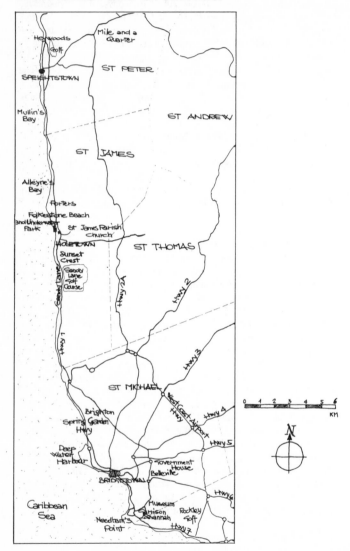

FOURTEEN

The west coast

Barbados is a paradise for beach lovers and you may well find it difficult to drag yourself away from relaxing under the palm trees, or snorkelling in the crystal-clear waters, to visit the "other Barbados" — but once you have started I am sure you will agree it was worth it. Certainly the best way to visit the island is to hire a car or Moke, but for those who do not wish to do this there are other solutions: coach tours, taxis or buses. Obviously buses do not offer the flexibility of car travel but the island does have a good bus service and the ride can be an adventure in itself! With its many hundreds of miles of surfaced roads Barbados lends itself to touring and most of the more important places of interest are clearly signposted. However, don't be surprised if you occasionally get lost — a friendly Barbadian will soon put you back on the right road — and you may make some interesting discovery on your detour.

This itinerary will accompany you along the west coast from Bridgetown to Speightstown, the island's second town. The route is well served by buses from Bridgetown for those who wish to use public transport.

Bridgetown to Holetown

From the centre of town take the Princess Alice Highway (parallel to the coast) and then **Spring Garden Highway** near the Deep Water Harbour. Spring Garden Highway has two reputations — of being the fastest road on the island (the speed limit is 80 kph!) and of being the venue of the Kadooment Day Parade. If you are on Barbados on the first Monday in August this is something not to be missed for Spring Garden takes on a carnival-like atmosphere with scores of little stalls, the latest calypso and soca favourites and the colourful street parade as the bands wind their way down from the National Stadium. On other days you will probably notice that the Highway is lined by more mundane sights, as this is one of the main poles of Barbados industrial development, especially at the southern end. Further north there is **Brighton** beach, a popular spot with the inhabitants of Bridgetown and the crowded townships of its suburbs. The end of the Highway is marked by a roundabout which leads onto the new ring road around the city and to the airport. Readers staying on the south coast will probably prefer to take the ring road and start the itinerary at this point.

At the roundabout we take the coast road, Highway 1, and head towards Holetown in the parish of St James. The road itself offers very little in way of scenery as it is generally built up on both sides, with a prevalence of up-market hotels on the left and a mixture of shops, restaurants and houses on the landward side. Traffic can be heavy, especially at rush hours, but the situation should be eased when the new Highway (the improved Highway 2A) is completed. This will link up Speightstown and the north with the city ring/airport road. At the time of writing work was under way.

Holetown

Under normal traffic conditions it will probably take you about a quarter of an hour to reach Holetown from the Spring Garden roundabout and, as you approach it, you will notice what is considered to be the island's leading property, the **Sandy Lane Hotel,** with its magnificent gardens on the left, and its 18-hole golf course on the right. The hotel was opened in 1961 and its success and fame was largely responsible for the development of the St James coast as one of the most desirable resort areas in the Caribbean. Shortly after the golf course, on your right, you will see the **Sunset Crest** shopping centre and residential area, while on your left you will find Holetown Police Station. Near the police station there is a monument to the early English settlers. It was here that John Powell landed on 14 May, 1625 and claimed the island in the name of the English Crown. Two years later the first settlers arrived at what was then known as St James' Town, perhaps a more attractive name than its present one which owes its origin to the safe anchorage the settlers found and which reminded them of 'The Hole' in the River Thames. It is interesting to note that whoever prepared the text for the monument, or who did the engraving, was certainly not top of the class at history for the inscription says the landing took place in 1605! Behind the police station lie the ruins of what was once James Fort — today only one solitary cannon remains to remind us of how well fortified this island was.

The Savannah Club overlooks the spacious ex-military parade ground, now given over to sport, on the outskirts of Bridgetown. Its tower has become a local landmark.

Holetown has one of the most attractive parish churches on the island — St James — which is located on the seaward side of the coast road. The church dates from 1847 but stands on the site of a previously existing church. The most important survivor of the early church, which probably dated from the pioneering days, is a bell dated 1699 and bearing the inscription 'God bless King William'. Today this can be found in the southern porch to the church. The church also contains a mural in memory of Sir John Gay Alleyne, a Speaker of the Barbadian House of Assembly in the late eighteenth century. Sir John was once the owner of the attractive Porters Great House, located in the vicinity of the Colony Club Hotel at Alleyne's Bay.

On the north side of the church, there is a lane that leads to **Folkestone Beach** and park. This is one of the few corridors of public access to the St James beaches. All the beaches in Barbados are public but unfortunately, on the west coast, access is rather limited owing to hotel and property development. Needless to say Folkestone is very popular with the locals, especially at the weekend. The beach is also the place to go if you want to visit the **Folkestone Underwater Park** — there are plenty of boats offering snorkellers and divers transport and equipment to the reef where an interesting trail has been laid out for divers to follow. Furthermore, Folkestone also offers the wreck of the ship *Stavronikita* which was deliberately sunk here to attract marine fauna and flora. Of course, for those who do not wish to do the exploring themselves, there are plenty of glass-bottom boats offering their services.

Next to the beach changing facilities, there is a small museum that houses exhibits on marine life and objects connected with the sea, while next door the Bellairs Research Institute carries out research on marine biology.

On to Speightstown

As you leave Holetown, near the Colony Club Hotel, you will see **Porters House,** mentioned before when we spoke of St James Church. The building is a fine example of an early plantation house, but it is not open to the public. Nearby, at **Heron Bay,** there is a modern (vintage 1947), but nonetheless imposing Palladian-style mansion. This was once the home of the late Ronald Tree, the Anglo-American who created the Sandy Lane Resort in the early 1960s and who did so much to preserve the island's heritage during his term of office as the President of the Barbados National Trust.

The coast road continues north along the 'Platinum Coast' with new luxury properties on the seaward side until it enters the parish of St Peter, just south of **Mullins Bay.** Here the road runs parallel to this popular beach before entering more ribbon development on the outskirts of Speightstown.

Speightstown

Speightstown is second in importance only to Bridgetown, and once indeed it had been considered as an alternative site for the capital. Today there is a modern by-pass round the town, so turn left for the town centre. If you miss the turning, don't worry, just turn left at the traffic light on the by-pass. The town was originally named after a Bristol merchant, William Speight. Speightstown became the main port in the north from which sugar was shipped to Bristol. The association between Speightstown and Bristol became so close that the former became known as 'Little Bristol'. The town became the main centre of the north of the island, with its shops, markets and services. In the past people from the northern parishes who wanted to travel to Bridgetown would take a boat from here. Today Speightstown still fulfils its role as a market and communciations centre but there is a sharp contrast between old and new. You will still see the little stores tucked away in the rather picturesque wooden buildings, with overhanging verandahs, in Church Street. Unfortunately, many of them are in a poor state of repair, but it is still posssible to imagine that the town had a certain old-world charm. In the midst of this, however, you will notice that twentieth-century development has not passed Speightstown by. You will find a modern shopping complex, complete with banks and a fast food restaurant, and the town sports a well-designed ultra-modern bus station that deserves top marks for its upkeep.

There is also a small promenade with seats under shady trees, a favourite spot with pensioners and others who just wish to 'lime' their time away. Nearby you will notice some of the cannons and what remains of the Denmark and Orange Forts which once defended the town. **St Peter's Parish Church** is the main place of worship and is located right in the centre, at the crossroads of Church and Queen Streets. Like many of Barbados's churches, it has been rebuilt more than once. The original building dates back to the 1630s, but it was rebuilt in 1837. In 1980 the church was gutted by a fire and restoration work took several years to complete. A further modern touch to the church is its electronic chiming clock — I believe I am not the only one who has his reservations on this matter!

Pico Teneriffe. View from Cove Bay on the St Lucy/St Peter boundary, a popular picnic site with Barbadians at the weekend.

FIFTEEN

St Peter and St Lucy

Speightstown, the main town of the north and the 'capital' of the parish of St Peter, has been considered in the chapter on the west coast. The present itinerary will deal with the inland areas of the parish of St Peter and the parish of St Lucy as a whole. You will not find tourist restaurants along the itinerary but there are some ideal places for a picnic lunch, and of course, you are never too far from a rum shop if you fancy joining the locals for a drink.

Starting from the traffic light on the Speightstown by-pass, we turn right up the hill in the direction of the village of **Mile and a Quarter.** The first part of this narrow road may be considered as an extension of Speightstown, with dozens of little wooden houses tumbling down the hill towards the road. A little later we pass St Joseph's Hospital on the left and then on to Mile and a Quarter. Here we keep on the main road and continue up the hill, past **All Saints' Church** (the present building dates from 1884 on the site of the original church built in the seventeenth century and destroyed in a hurricane in 1831), until we meet the junction with the new highway.

'Island in the Sun'

This fine new trunk road links the east coast with St Lucy and was largely built for the lorries carrying sand to the Arawak Cement Plant on the St Lucy coast. We turn right and keep on this main highway through the St Peter sugar belt and then up the hill to **Farley Hill National Park.** This is located at the brow of the hill, on the right of the road (small admission charge for cars). Farley Hill is the site of what was one of the most sumptuous houses on

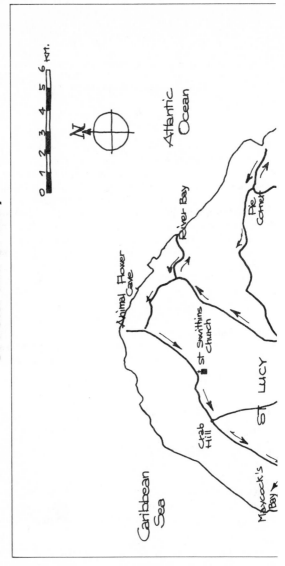

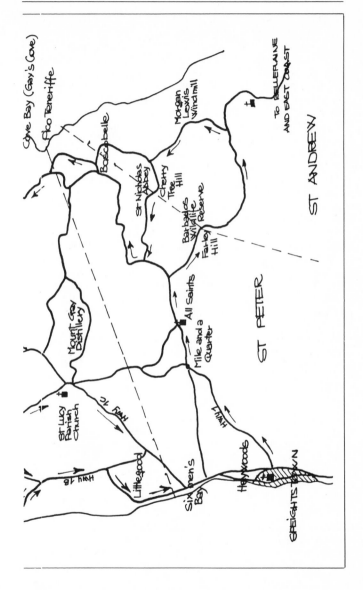

the island, the ruins of which can be still seen, but is essentially a well-cared for park, with spectacular views over the north and east of the island. The house was originally known as Grenade Hall, the oldest part of which dates back to 1818. However, it was Thomas Graham Briggs (later known as Sir Graham Briggs) who added the south wing in the 1850s and who renamed the house 'Farley Hill'. Briggs owned large sugar estates in St Peter and Christ Church and spent much of the profits on embellishing Farley Hill and its gardens and entertaining distinguished visitors, including Queen Victoria's second son, Prince Alfred. After Briggs's death the house passed into the hands of the Howell family and then for many years remained empty. By now Barbados was in the midst of a long depression and nobody was interested in spending money to restore such a residence, particularly considering the distance from Bridgetown. The house did have a brief moment of glory, however, when in 1956 it was used for the setting of the film *Island in the Sun*. Unfortunately it was the very material that was used for restoring the house for the film that was to provide the fuel for the fire which was to destroy the house a few years later. In 1965, however, the Government decided to purchase the property and declared it a National Park. The Queen unveiled a plaque here during a visit to the island in 1966. Today the park has been beautifully restored and is a popular spot with Barbadians and visitors alike. The old house still stands in ruins but it is not improbable that one day this will be restored to its former glory and serve as a museum or a conference centre.

Monkeys galore

On the opposite side of the main road to Farley Hill (which, by the way, can also be reached by public transport) we find the **Barbados Wildlife Reserve** (open daily 10.00 am to 5.00 pm — admission charge at time of writing BDS$8). The Reserve is situated in a mahogany wood and is primarily a monkey sanctuary, offering the visitor excellent opportunities to photograph the monkeys in their natural environment. It also boasts a walk-through aviary and hosts a number of other animals, such as tortoises, otters, wallabies and caymans. The Reserve is a result of work of the Barbados Primate Research Center, whose aims include the preservation of the island's green monkey population. Monkeys are often considered pests by farmers for the damage they cause to crops and one of the Center's functions is to help farmers by capturing monkeys and keeping their numbers down to reasonable levels. The argument for this is that large numbers of the 'pests' would lead farmers to retaliate drastically and there would be the risk of the monkeys being driven into extinction. The captured monkeys are exported to foreign zoos and for medical research on vaccines.

A windmill and a Great House

The highway now descends quickly towards the Atlantic coast and the Scotland District of the parish of St Andrew, passing on the way the old Cleland sugar factory. At the bottom of the hill, at the T-junction, turn left for the village of Storey and the **Morgan Lewis Windmill.** The windmill is a National Trust property and has been beautifully restored. This mill is not particularly old, having been built only at the turn of the century, and was operational until the 1940s, but it is a reminder of what the Barbados landscape must have been like when there were hundreds of windmills used for crushing sugar-cane, and it is also a tribute to the Dutch who introduced sugar technology to the island in the seventeenth century.

We continue up the steep hill, inappropriately known as **Cherry Tree Hill,** for the only trees are mahogany. The brow of the hill offers a fine view over the Scotland District and the east coast — normally there are a few 'guides' around, waiting to point out the places of interest and perhaps to sell you a sample of sugar-cane. The road is now covered by a shady canopy of mahogany trees and shortly afterwards we find the well-signposted lane for **St Nicholas Abbey.** Don't be misled by the name, for there is no abbey but one of the oldest Great Houses in Barbados, dating from between 1650 and 1660. The picturesque house with its three curved gables and chimneys certainly looks rather out of place in a tropical setting, but gives us an indication of the wealth that abounded among the seventeenth-century plantocracy. The ground floor of the property is open to visitors (10.00 am to 3.30 pm Mondays to Fridays) who will be conducted around the two panelled reception rooms with some fine examples of eighteenth- and nineteenth-century furniture. At the back of the house there is a Chinese Chippendale staircase, with the panel design changing as you ascend. Other points of interest include some examples of Wedgwood pottery, on loan from the Barbados Museum, extracts from a slave register and some photographs of the sugar plantation in the 1830s. There is also an interesting film show (at 11.30 and 2.30) portraying life in Barbados in the 1930s. The house has been the property of the Cave family since 1832 but the present owner and gracious host, Lieutenant-Colonel Stephen Cave, is the first member of the family to use the house as his permanent home.

The rugged north-east

Leaving St Nicholas Abbey we travel westwards to Diamond Corner and then turn right at the T-junction to Boscobelle and Pie Corner. Boscobelle is the village nearest the tiny wedge of St Peter on the Atlantic coast, where there is a pyramid-like cliff known as **Pico Teneriffe.** However, the best place to photograph the cliff and this rugged coastline is from **Cove Bay** (or Gay's Cove on the map), a favourite picnic spot with Barbadians at weekends. The way to Cove Bay is to turn right at Pie Corner and then, when you reach a ranch-style house, take a track on the right, across the field to the coconut grove — and you have arrived!

Another popular site for weekend excursionists on this north-east coast is **River Bay,** where you will find the bay and the dry river-bed cut into the hills, shady casuarina trees and changing facilities. As at most places on the east coast you should be very careful about swimming because of the waves and the currents — so beware, never be attracted by deserted beaches.

Animal flower cave

One of the features of the St Lucy coastline (Boscobelle was the last village in St Peter) is that there is a lunar-like setting for the land near the sea — semi-abandoned scrub with a few black-bellied sheep and goats grazing. A good example of this is the approach to our next destination, **Animal Flower Cave.** This is located near **North Point,** the most northerly tip of the island and is well-signposted from St Lucy's Parish Church. Arriving from River Bay and Pie Corner, take the road signposted for the church and fork right when you arrive at the main road)Highway 1C). There is a small entrance fee to the caves for which a guide is provided. The main attraction to the caves are the sea anemones in the rock pools which indeed look like flowers, hence the name, and the roaring surf at the entrance to the cave. Once outside you may like to take some refreshment in the bar run by Manuel and Pancho Ward. An unusual feature of this simple building is that the owners have saved on wallpapering costs by building up the biggest collection of visiting cards on the island. Your card will be very welcome! North Point offers fine views over the merging Atlantic and Caribbean and is a favourite spot with seasoned surfers, as is Duppies, a little further west, near the village of Crab Hill.

More coast and a distillery

Taking the main road westwards from Animal Flower Cave, we pass St Swithins Church and Crab Hill Police Station, where there is a junction. If we keep straight on at the junction we arrive at the west coast of St Lucy while the left turn leads to St Lucy's Parish Church, and from there to the Mount Gay rum distillery, or straight back to Speightstown.

The most attractive bay on St Lucy's west coast is undoubtedly **Maycock's Bay,** bordered at the northern end by the lighthouse and Barbados Defence Force base at Harrison's Point while the Arawak Cement Plant lies to the south. And while an industrial plant and an army base do not sound like ideal neighbours, Maycock still offers a beautiful cliff-lined bay with access to the shore and the ruins of an old fort. To reach the bay you must take one of the by-ways off the main road near Bromefield or Maycock. Continuing along the main road we turn right at Checker Hall, proceed down the hill and then follow the coast through the sleepy fishing villages of **Littlegood** and **Six Men's Bay** back to Speightstown. Six Men's Bay was once important for whaling, an activity that has long been abandoned in most of the Caribbean. Today you will find a few fishing boats pulled up on the beach under the manchineel trees. The manchineel is one of the perils on Barbadian beaches (sea urchins being the other) — the little green manchineel apples are not only poisonous but they will burn and blister your skin if you shelter under the tree in rain. In the more tourist-beaten areas there is a danger warning or a red ring painted on the offending tree.

The alternative route is from Crab Tree Police Station to **St Lucy's Parish Church.** Like many of the island's churches, it dates back to the early days of colonisation (1629 in fact), only to be destroyed in a hurricane (1821) and then reconstructed. The church is a focal point for the whole of a parish with a sparse rural population. Opposite the church, just north of the new roundabout, we find the road that leads to one of the island's most famous rum distilleries, **Mount Gay.** If you wish to visit the distillery it is open to visitors, with two daily tours at 11.00 and 2.30, Monday to Friday, except in August when it is closed for maintenance. The product is not matured at Mount Gay, but at Brandons, near Bridgetown. Those who would like to learn more about rum may be interested in the weekly luncheon tour (usually on Wednesdays), called 'Where the Rum Come From', held at the Bridgetown distillery (tel. 435-6900 for reservations).

To return to Speightstown and the west coast from St Lucy roundabout, you can either fork left for the new highway and then turn right for Mile and a Quarter and Speightstown, or take the old road down to Littlegood Harbour.

SIXTEEN

The centre and the east

This itinerary may be considered the nature-lover's itinerary par excellence, including as it does several tropical gardens, the only piece of virgin forest left on the island, spectacular caves and the beautiful, breezy Atlantic coast, exposed to the trade winds and the pounding surf. Probably you will find it all a bit too much for one day and may well be advised to sample the gardens, for example, on different days. I have put them together here as one itinerary for their geographical location.

St Thomas

St Thomas is one of the two parishes (the other being St George) that is entirely landlocked. It is essentially 'sugar country', with the red soils of the plateau area, cut by occasional gullies. There are several roads from the west and the south into the parish, but for the purpose of this itinerary we shall use Highway 2, starting from Warrens Roundabout on the new West Coast-Airport Highway. The roundabout can be conveniently reached from Bridgetown and from the west and south without entering the city.

The Moravians

The first place of interest en route is **Sharon Moravian Chapel** which was built in 1765. The visitor will note that its architecture is very different from the island's Anglican parish churches and the architect was clearly influenced by the style of Central Europe, with its characteristic tower and windows. The Moravians, along with the Methodists, were the two Protestant churches that did most for the well-being of the slaves. The Anglican Church, it must be

The centre and the east

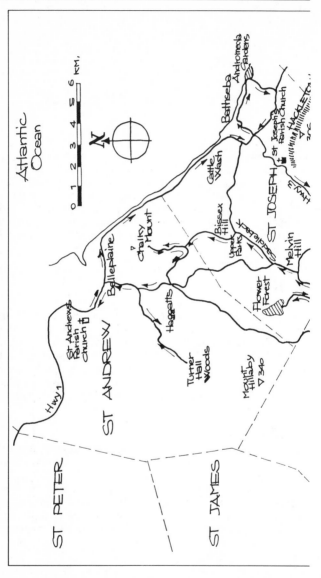

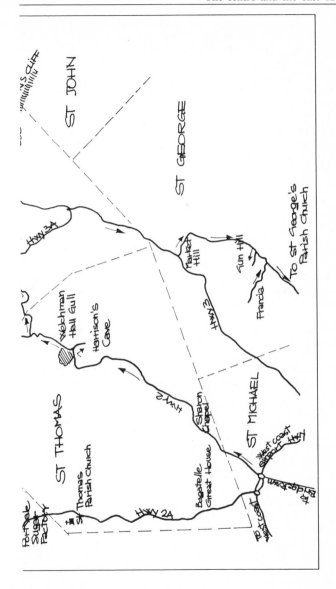

remembered, did not even allow the baptism of slaves in this period. Not surprisingly this has left its mark and today there is still a sizable Moravian community on the island.

The Gully and the Caves

Our next stop is at **Welchman Hall Gully,** a luxuriant crack in the island's limestone cap which provides over a kilometre of tropical vegetation offering a profusion of flowers, fruit and spice trees, as well as a gigantic pillar formed of the fusion of a stalactite and a stalagmite. The gully took its name from a Welsh family who once owned the property and who, in the mid-nineteenth century, tried to transform the ravine into a fruit and nutmeg grove. The adventure was then abandoned with the result that the gully grew wild again. After decades of neglect the property was taken over by the National Trust in the 1960s and transformed into a unique natural park.

Across the main road from the gully you will find the approach road to one of the island's leading attractions — **Harrison's Cave.** The existence of the caves had been known for many years but it was only in 1970 that a Danish speleologist discovered the entrance to the gigantic cavern (75 metres long by 30 wide and high) and other underground splendours. The Government decided to invest in the site as a unique tourist attraction (the only one of its kind in the Caribbean) and opened up tunnels for an electric tram, installed indirect lighting and provided a fine reception area, complete with an exhibit of Arawak artefacts. As a limited number of visitors can be taken round the cave at one time (the tour lasts about an hour), advance booking is essential, especially if there are cruise ships in port. There is a brief slide-show introduction to the caves, followed by the tram ride. The experience is indeed a memorable one as you pass bubbling streams, thundering waterfalls, gigantic stalactites and stalagmites. The cave is open seven days a week — first tour 9.00 am, last tour 4.00 pm — for reservations call 438-6640 or 438-6641. Entrance BDS$10.

Some alternative places of interest

For readers who do not plan to continue on the rest of the itinerary, but who are perhaps interested in only a half day excursion, I would like to suggest one or two places of interest in the parish of St Thomas. Return to Warrens Roundabout, turn right and continue

Saturday afternoon entertainment — a Bajan cricket match.

as far as the next roundabout and then take Highway 2A. After a few kilometres you will arrive at **Bagatelle Great House.** This is one of the oldest houses on the island, vying with Drax Hall and St Nicholas Abbey for the title. Bagatelle originally belonged to Lord Willoughby, one of the earliest Governors of Barbados, and was known until the 1870s as Parnham Park House. Lord Willoughby was the king's representative in 1650, in the stormy days of the Civil War in England. Cromwell sent his 'task force' to purge this Royalist stronghold and after resisting for some time the island was forced to surrender, but on honourable terms. Lord Willoughby returned to England and was later imprisoned for plotting against the Government. However, when Charles II regained the throne, Lord Willoughby was rewarded for his loyalty by being made Governor of Barbados again. The Willoughby family lost the property in 1877 as part of a gambling debt. Today the house accommodates one of the most refined and expensive restaurants on the island.

A few minutes later you will arrive at **St Thomas Parish Church** which has the unenviable record of being the church that has been most damaged by hurricanes, having been completely destroyed in 1675, 1780 and 1831. Like many Barbadian parish churches it is located at a cross-roads, and seemingly in the middle of nowhere. A left turn here will lead you to Holetown and the west coast, whereas if you continue a short distance along Highway 2A you will come to the **Portvale Sugar Machinery Museum,** just over the border in the parish of St James. This is located on the site of a working sugar factory and visitors interested in the sugar-making process will be able to glean a lot of information from the attendant who has had many years experience in the industry. There is a nominal entrance fee.

St Joseph and St Andrew

The Flower Forest

Continuing our route from Harrison's Cave, a short distance north of the access road to the cave, take a right turning for the **Flower Forest** and follow the signposts along the bumpy narrow lanes into the uplands of St Joseph. The Flower Forest is a well-landscaped tropical garden located on what was once the Richmond Estate, high up on the fringe of the Scotland District. The gardens were opened only in 1983 so some of the trees and plants are still rather young, but nonetheless very attractive and well labelled. Here you will be able to see a good selection of tropical fruits from bananas to soursop. Be sure to have plenty of film, because besides the gardens there are fine views over the Scotland District. The Flower Forest is open daily from 9.00 am to 5.00 pm (entrance BDS$8).

The Saddleback route

The next part of the route follows some of the most scenic roads on the island, known locally as **The Saddleback.** The roads are very steep at times, narrow and not always in the greatest of shape — i.e. watch out for potholes — so if you don't feel that you or your vehicle are up to it, play safe and take the alternative route along Highway 2. To get to the Saddleback from the Flower Forest turn left (instead of right for Highway 2) and keep bearing left to the village of Melvin Hill, then take the right fork at Upper Parks for

The rugged lunar-like scenery of North Point (St Lucy) where the Atlantic meets the Carribean.

Bissex Hill, where you have the choice of the rapid descent to Bathsheba on the east coast (right fork) or a visit to the **Potteries of Chalky Mount** (left fork). If you wish to visit Chalky Mount using the alternative route, turn right near Haggatts Agricultural Station — the last part of the route is steep and narrow in any case. Chalky Mount is an isolated community of potters and here you will be able to watch the skilled craftsmen at work on their treddle machines. An abundant supply of local clay and a tradition going back many generations has led to a trade in pot-making. Many of the finished articles are glazed and can make original souvenirs at affordable prices.

Orchards and woods

Backtracking from Chalky Mount to Highway 2, you may be interested in the **Barbados cherry tree orchard** near the road at Haggatts Agricultural Station. The fruit of this tree is said to have one of the highest concentrations of Vitamin C in the world. The Research Station is helping to promote the cultivation of the fruit on the island and the export of trees. The Station also has an important nursery supplying citrus and mango trees as part of the Government's diversification policy and as a means of preventing land slippage and erosion, a serious problem in the Scotland District after heavy rains.

Shortly after Haggatts, on your left, you will find the minor road that leads to **Turner Hall Woods.** This small remote wooded area — its remoteness being responsible for its very survival — is today the only primaeval forest on the island. There is a mixed assortment of trees ranging from the 30-metre tall, straight locust trees to red cedar, mastic, cabbage palm and jack-in-the-box bearing their fruit in a sort of hollow bladder. When the English settlers first arrived on the island most of Barbados was covered with such vegetation, but already by the Sugar Revolution, just a few decades later, most woodland had been cleared.

The Belleplaine district

Belleplaine at the junction of Highway 2 and the East Coast Road is the main settlement in the Scotland District, providing such services as schools, a police station, a petrol station and a store or two. It was also the last station of the much missed Barbados Railway (1881-1938) which crossed the island from Bridgetown to Bathsheba and Belleplaine, the journey taking several hours! George Lamming, Barbados's leading novelist, describes his boyhood

experience of the railway in his classic *In the Castle of my Skin:*
'The small boys waited in the wood listening cautiously for the
rhythm of the wheels along the lines, and peering through the trees
and away in the distance for a whiff of steam shot from the carcass
of the engine. They crouched at intervals of five, three, four yards.
On the lines the metal pins beamed. The flames caught and crashed
in the wind. The boys slouching at a safe distance from the
railtracks watched where the metal seemed to set the lines aflame.
On this bright morning so much depended on the pins. Here the
boys had set the adventure of the day, and soon in a collision of
lines and metal and wheels the life of a knife or several knives would
be formed.'

If you visit Sunbury Plantation House (see the itinerary covering
the south), you will find some pictures of the railway.

Before turning right for the east coast, it is worth making a short
detour and driving north to **St Andrew's Parish Church,** located just
outside Belleplaine. This attractive church was built in 1842 —
ironically the original church, unlike most Bajan churches, had
survived the terrible hurricane in 1831 but then fell into such
disrepair that it had to be demolished.

The east coast

Returning to the Belleplaine junction, we now take the wide East
Coast Road that runs parallel to the surf-pounded beach from
Lakes Beach to Cattlewash. Many would consider this to be the
most beautiful road on the island, with its backdrop of Chalky
Mount and pasturing cows and sheep, the odd holiday house or two
and the well-kept picnic area at Barclays Park with its beach
facilities. The only blemish on this perfect setting is that in most
places the sea conditions are dangerous for swimming. There is a
lifeguard service, however, at **Cattlewash** at the far end of the
beach. Here at the side of the main road you will find the attractive
colonial-style Kingsley Club which offers excellent local food and is
a popular lunchtime stopping point where diners sit behind jalousied
windows on the breezy verandah. This is the type of inn you will
not find in any tour brochure but you might wish you could!

After Cattlewash the road makes a sharp right turn and becomes
narrow and steep and soon you will arrive at a rather dangerous
cross-roads — watch out for cars shooting across the brow, many
a hand-brake won't hold on the extremely steep road coming up

from the left. Right for Bridgetown, straight on for St John and left for Bathsheba.

Bathsheba

Bathsheba is the main east coast settlement nestling along the shoreline and backing up the steep hill. On maps it is often given the same importance as Oistins, Holetown or Speightstown, but in reality it is a very small settlement. For those without their own transport Bathsheba can make an ideal bus outing, being served by buses both from Bridgetown and Speightstown. By taking three buses (Bridgetown-Bathsheba, Bathsheba-Speightstown and Speightstown-Bridgetown) you can have a mini-tour of the island for just three dollars! At the far end of the village you will find rocks stretching out in the sea with foaming surf — the surfing championships are held at Bathsheba in September — and beyond the rocks the little fishing fleet of **Tent Bay** bobbing at anchor. Overlooking the bay we find the Atlantis Hotel, a small guesthouse that is one of the oldest hotels on the island. This too is a popular spot at lunchtimes when it can get quite crowded with tour passengers.

Nearby, just a little up the hill, you will find the famous **Andromeda Gardens,** a National Trust property that is one of the finest botanical gardens in the whole Caribbean. These were the life-long work and passion of their creator, the late Mrs Iris Bannochie, taking their mythological name from their cliff setting. The work was started in 1954 and has never stopped as the gardens are constantly being transformed and expanded. Imagination has never been lacking in the landscaping and landuse. The array of colour is magnificent from frangipani, bignonia and hibiscus. The micro-climates, maybe of just a few square feet, have been exploited to the full, ensuring that each plant grows in its ideal conditions. The pride and joy of Andromeda, however, is the orchid garden with orchids growing in pots under exotic fruit trees. Trees and plants have been imported from all over the world, but today this is no longer a one-way traffic and Andromeda has become an exporter of Barbadian beauty. The gardens are open daily from 6 am to 6 pm.

Opposite: *The calm waters and the fine sandy beach of the west coast provide an ideal spot for a swim.*

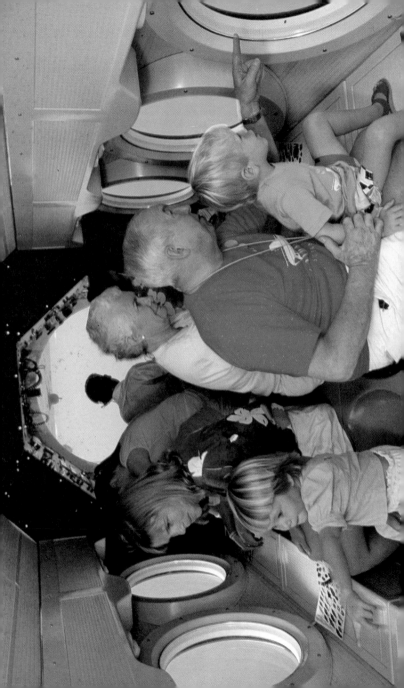

St George — north

Gun Hill

To return to the Bridgetown area, head back towards the Bathsheba cross-roads mentioned before, and make your way up Horse Hill on Highway 3 and then on through the last corner of St Joseph into the fertile sugar-cane parish of St George. Just off the main road near Market Hall, you will find one of the parish's greatest claims to fame, **Gun Hill.** It is signposted but you may miss the turning on your way down the hill. If you arrive at the parish church, you have come too far! Gun Hill is the highest spot in the district and is known for its signal station and its Imperial Lion. The former is a look-out point on top of the hill, offering fantastic views over all the south of the island. It is easy to understand why it became a signal station. Today it has been beautifully restored by the National Trust and is worth a visit not only for the views but also for maps and pictures explaining the workings of the island's pre-telegraphic communications system. This was used to warn of dangers, both from enemy attack and slave revolts, and depended on a system of signal towers strung on high points round the island. Further along the one-way lane you will find another reminder of the British military presence, the limestone lion sculpted in 1868 by Henry Wilkinson, a British Army officer. Underneath, in Latin, there is a suitable jingoistic inscription, which translates as follows: 'It (the British Lion) shall rule from the rivers to the sea, and from the sea to the ends of the earth.'

Opposite: *(Courtesy Atlantis Submarine) The Atlantis submarine — visitors find this unique experience of visiting the depths of the Caribbean one of the highlights of their Bajan stay. Be sure to take fast (1000 ASA) film with you.*

A fine plantation house

Proceed a little further down the hill and you will see a turning signposted **Francia,** which is one of the island's more recent Great Houses. Francia is set at the edge of a mahogany wood and is surrounded by beautiful gardens and extensive lawns. The house was built at the turn of the century by a Frenchman who had moved to Barbados from Brazil, and its features include its inset gallery and half Demerara shutters. Its impressive entrance hall is panelled with Brazilian wood. Besides its fine mahogany furniture it boasts a collection of old maps, including one of Barbados dated 1657. Here you will also see the originals of the prints you saw at Gun Hill Signal Station. Francia is open daily Mondays through Fridays, except public holidays. Admission charge BDS$6.

The parish church

We can now backtrack to the main road and continue the return journey down Gun Hill to **St George's Parish Church.** The church was built in 1784 and, unlike most other churches, survived the terrible hurricane of 1831. The altar piece representing the resurrection was painted by the American artist, Benjamin West. Legend has it that the centurion's eye was damaged by a thief who didn't like being watched while he committed his crime. Shortly after the church we join Highway 4 at Salters before regaining the by-pass at Rouen.

SEVENTEEN

The south

This last itinerary will take us to the four southern parishes of St John, St. Philip, Christ Church and the part of St George not dealt with in the preceding chapter. The parish of St John has its own distinctive character, with Hackleton's Cliff that divides it into two; St George and St Philip are essentially flat sugar-cane lands that offer opulent Great Houses testifying to the wealth this area once produced; while the populous parish of Christ Church offers a mix of suburbia, the tourist industry, fishing and an extension of the southern sugar-cane lands.

St George — south

Our starting point will be St Barnabas roundabout on the West Coast-Airport Highway where we find Karl Broodhagen's famous statue 'The Freed Slave' erected to commemorate the 150th anniversary of the abolition of slavery. The figure representing Bussa, one of the leaders of the 1816 slave revolt, holds his head back with pride while his wrists bear the broken chains. We travel north along the Highway and then turn right onto Highway 4 at the Rouen roundabout. This leads us into the rich 'sugar lands' of the St George Valley. As we proceed eastwards we will pass Bulkley sugar factory. At present there are only six sugar factories on the island and there is talk of further rationalisation as sugar-cane production continues to decline. If you are passing in the grinding season (February-May) you may like to drop in and watch operations.

The South

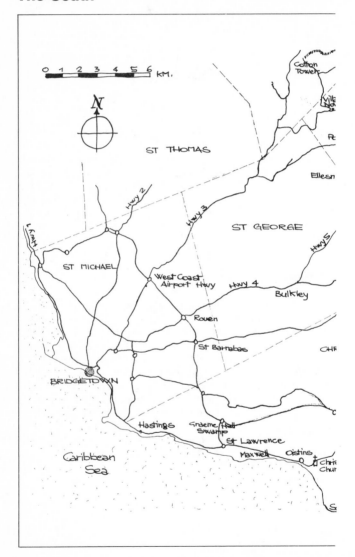

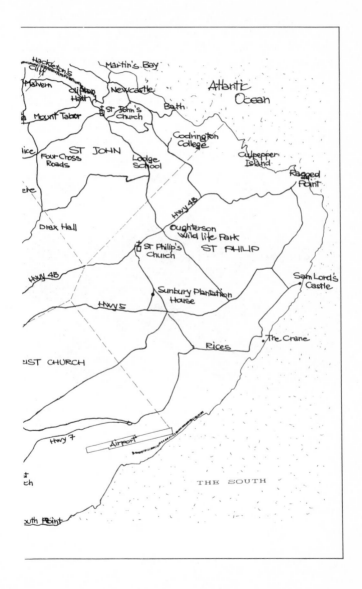

Not far after Bulkley the road forks and we take the left fork to continue on Highway 4. After a few minutes we arrive at the drive of one of the most famous and oldest plantation houses on the island — **Drax Hall.** This fine Jacobean Great House (probably dating from the 1650s), with its steep gables, is hidden from the road by trees. Drax Hall, which is still in the hands of the Drax family, is normally closed to the public, except occasionally during the National Trust's special Great House Programme in winter. If you are fortunate enough to visit it you will note that the house is enhanced by a particularly fine example of a Jacobean staircase, while the carved archway leading from the entrance to the staircase is in mastic wood, a variety of timber no longer found on the island.

Tent Bay, Batsheba. A favourite holiday spot with old Bajan families. Swimming on the east coast is dangerous in many places and should be practised only at beaches with a lifeguard.

St John

Shortly after Drax Hall you will find a junction, with a secondary road on the left leading to Ellesmere and Four Cross Roads in the parish of St John. We leave Highway 4 and proceed along this secondary road until it meets Highway 3B near St John's police station. Cross over Highway 3 and continue along the secondary road for two or three kilometres (forking left near Mount Tabor Church) until you reach Villa Nova.

Villa Nova

Villa Nova is considered one of the finest examples of a nineteenth-century Great House. The house was built in the 1830s on a one thousand acre (four hundred hectare) sugar estate belonging to the Haynes family, but the house and the estate were separated in 1907. For almost sixty years the house remained the property of the Government and was assigned to the Medical Officer of St John as his home and surgery before former British Prime Minister, the Earl of Avon, purchased Villa Nova as his winter home. Because of deteriorating health the Earl sold the house in 1971. The house was then bought by Mr and Mrs Ernest Hunte who in their sixteen years of residence did much to enrich Villa Nova's furnishings by adding a fine collection of mahogany antiques. The present owners, who wish to remain anonymous, have had the house since 1987. The lawns and gardens of this elevated corner of St John are particularly pleasant with wild orchids creeping up an assortment of mahogany and fruit trees. The house is usually open from 9.00 am to 4.00 pm Mondays to Fridays (it is advisable to telephone in advance, the number is 433-1524). Admission BDS$6.

The church on the cliff

Although Villa Nova is in a relatively high position (over 250 metres) you do not have an impression of height, except for the mitigating heat, but by taking the lane due north from Mount Tabor Church our impression will soon be corrected. The lane leads to the village of Malvern and **Hackleton's Cliff,** the 300-metre (almost one thousand feet) high cliff which marks the escarpment of the central upland plateau that extends from St Joseph's to St John's parish churches. From here you will have extensive views of the east coast from Pico Teneriffe in the north to Ragged Point Lighthouse in the south. Directly below you will notice luxuriant vegetation that hides the access to caves which were once the hideaways of runaway slaves and indentured servants. If you turn left at the western edge of the cliff you will find the **Cotton Tower,** a signal tower that has been restored by the National Trust. The Tower offers excellent views over the Scotland District of St Joseph. If we backtrack to Malvern, and then continue along the lane to Clifton Hall (where there is another fine estate house but which is not open to the public), we eventually arrive at **St John's Parish Church.**

St John's is considered one of the most unusual churches on the island and is certainly the one that is most visited by tourists. There are several factors that contribute to this, not least being its magnificent position, perched on the cliff top. The churchyard offers breath-taking views over the east coast and the villages below the cliff. The little cemetery also contains the tomb of Ferdinando Paleologus, a descendent of the Byzantine Imperial family who had to flee Constantinople to escape massacre by the Turks. Apparently he fought on the Royalist side in the English Civil War and then came to Barbados as a refugee. He lived in the parish of St John until his death in 1678.

The church itself dates from 1660 but the original building was destroyed in the terrible hurricane of 1831 and the present building was erected in 1836. Inside you will note the double staircase that leads to the organ gallery, the fine pulpit and an unusual sculpture of the Madonna and Child with the infant St John. If you attend the service on a Sunday morning it is difficult to imagine that once this church would have been reserved for whites, the rich planters at the front and the poor whites at the back. The only reminder of the plantocracy today is their tombstones.

The 'Red legs'

The villages of **Newcastle, Martin's Bay** and **Bath,** nestling below the Cliff were once known for their 'Red leg' community. The 'Red legs' or poor whites are the descendents of the indentured servants who went to Barbados in the seventeenth century. They constituted a very mixed group, some being volunteers who agreed to be tied to one master for a period of from five to seven years to repay their passage and to have the opportunity of starting a new life as settlers, others were refugees and prisoners of war (from the English Civil War), others were criminals or prostitutes sent to the colonies as their punishment, while still other unfortunates were simply kidnapped or 'barbadosed' and smuggled aboard the waiting ships. Whatever their origin, they all faced terrible conditions once they arrived on the island, being treated little better than the

St John's parish church (St John). One of the island's most attractive churches, with fine views over the Atlantic from the churchyard where Ferdinando Paleologus, a descendant of the Imperial line of the last Christian emperors of Greece, is buried.

slaves, sweltering under the tropical sun (hence the name 'Red legs' from their peeling skin — some would say that many were Scottish and wore kilts). After the Sugar Revolution there was no longer

Fishing boats pulled up on the shore at Tent Bay, near Batsheba.

room or need for poor whites and many of them emigrated to North America whilst those who remained sank into ever deepening misery. They eked out a living by subsistence farming and by joining the militia which was used to prevent slave rebellions. They felt superior because of the colour of their skin and did not marry with blacks or coloureds. This inbreeding led to a sickly apathetic group who, with the aboliton of slavery, lost what little incentive they had had. Today you will find the remnants of this community concentrated in the villages of St John. Those who have remained are farmers or fishermen but others have left for the city and have been successfully integrated into Barbadian society.

If you would like to learn more about this beautiful area of St John and the history of its people, you may be interested in joining one of the full-day hikes organised by the Outdoor Club of Barbados. The Club's actvities includes promoting the area but at the same time preserving its natural beauty and heritage.

One of the villages mentioned above, Bath, offers one of the few safe bathing spots on the east coast, with changing facilities and a shady picnic area. In sharp contrast to this seemingly isolated corner you will notice the external communications centre with its satellite dish scanning the skies. The centre assures the island instant access to all parts of the world and fosters the development of new industry such as data processing and financial services.

Old schools

The parish of St John also hosts two of the island's oldest educational institutions — **Codrington College** and **Lodge School.** Both institutions were founded as the result of the will of one man, Christopher Codrington, a rich planter who bequeathed his property and slaves to an Anglican missionary society on his death in 1710. Codrington intended that the legacy should be used to Christianise and educate negroes, who in those days were considered little more than beasts by planters and clergy alike. Not surprisingly therefore, the scheme came in for a lot of opposition from both groups and it was not until 1745 that Codrington Grammar School (later known as Lodge School) and Codrington College were established. For many years, however, the institutions did not respect the conditions of the will, namely for the education and training of missionaries, but instead they became schools for the children of the Barbadian gentry. The theology college, which is today an integral part of the University of the West Indies, is located near Sealy Hall, to the south of Bath. The long drive, lined with gigantic cabbage palms, is indeed an impressive sight, as is the building itself, with its uncompleted quadrangle and its fine chapel. Lodge School, which is today one of the island's top secondary schools, is located further inland from the college.

St Philip

If we continue southwards we enter the parish of St Philip and arrive at a T-junction (Highway 4B). A detour to the left will take us to the most easterly of the island's lighthouses near **Ragged**

Point, whose solitary cliffs overlook the Atlantic, and, to the north, tiny Culpepper Island which is located only thirty metres or so from the mainland. Otherwise we can turn right along Highway 4B as far as the cross-roads near the police station. We turn left and soon we will see the signs for **Oughterson Wildlife Park.** Here American environmentalist Bill Miller has created a Nature Trail along which you will see several rare species of birds being bred in captivity and a variety of animals and reptiles. The Park is set on an old sugar-cane plantation and today it still operates as a farm specialising in poultry-rearing and fruit production.

Sunbury

A little further on a minor road on the right leads to the settlement of Padmore and **Sunbury Plantation House.** If you prefer to arrive at Sunbury by a better road you can always backtrack to Highway 4B and then turn left at St Philip's Parish Church. Sunbury Plantation House was once part of the extensive Sunbury Plantation, but today the two are separate. This very attractive house dates back to the 1660s when the property was originally known as 'Chapmans', much of the stone for the building having been brought from England as ballast. After various improvements over the years, in 1777 the estate was purchased by the Barrow family and renamed 'Sunbury'. In 1981 the house was bought by Keith and Angela Melville who restored it and opened the museum of carriages and old plantation equipment in what had once been the yam cellars. Today Sunbury is the lived-in home of Sally and Nicholas Thomas who once a week offer visitors the opportunity to sample an exclusive dinner (not more than 14 can be seated around the 200-year-old mahogany table) with a very refined menu, wine, after-dinner drinks and transport being included in the price. Daytime visitors, on the other hand, may well be tempted to enjoy the excellent lunches and teas served in the attractive courtyard restaurant — don't forget to try the coconut pie! — after having visited the splendidly furnished house (including the bedrooms) and the museum. Among the pieces of furniture of note are the planter's desk with its many pigeon holes and a pair of Berbice chairs with two mobile foot rests, the lady's model having the foot rest at a lower, more discreet level. Sunbury is open daily (except Sundays) 10 am - 4.30 pm, admission BDS$8.

Gun Hill Station (St George). A recently renovated signal tower offers fine views over the south of the island. It was one of a network of such towers that were used to send semaphor signals across the island to give warnings of enemy attack or slave revolts.

A pirate's castle

One of the items you will undoubtedly be shown at Sunbury is the personal claret set that once belonged to Sam Lord, a regency gentleman with the reputation of being a pirate. The mansion Lord had built on his illicit gains can been seen a few miles away and is known as **Sam Lord's Castle.** The Castle is well signposted so you should have no dificulty reaching it from Sunbury, the easiest route being along Highway 5 and turning right at the end. Today the Castle is part of the large Marriot's resort which uses the original Georgian mansion as the reception area and 10 guest rooms. The building was started in 1820 and completed in 1833 by Lord's own slave labour force. It has crenellated battlements, hence the name 'castle' and originally there were open verandahs on all sides. No expense was spared on the interior decorating — Lord employed only the best craftsmen available, for example the fine plaster ceilings were designed by Charles Rutter who had designed ceilings for Windsor Castle. Other features include the domed ceiling above the staircase and the handsome woodwork. The drawing- and dining-rooms contain some fine antique furniture and paintings, including a portrait of the Duke of York by Sir Joshua Reynolds. Take a stroll across the lawns and at the bottom of the garden you will have a view over the wooded beach where it is claimed Lord hung lanterns on the trees to attract ships on to the rocks of Cobblers Reef. The fact that Lord was absent when some of the ships were wrecked would lead us to believe that his reputation might have been exaggerated, to say the least, but his legend lives on.

The Crane

Another fine hotel on the St Philip coast, and one of the oldest on the island, lies a few kilometres to the south-west at Crane Beach. The hotel of the same name is perched on the low cliffs overlooking the magnificent beach — beware of bathing, however, because of the dangerous currents. But to compensate for this the Crane offers an unusual Roman-style swimming pool. By the way, the name the 'Crane' is derived from the fact that there used to be a crane here for loading ships. We should remember that in the past coastal transport was very common in Barbados owing to the precarious state of the roads.

Christ Church

A fishing village

Travelling inland from the Crane, past Rices, we turn left to join the road that leads to Grantley Adams International Airport. Here we should bear left for Highway 7 which will lead us to the chief town of the parish of Christ Church, Oistins. **Oistins** was originally a fishing village nestling round the bay of the same name, but today has grown considerably and offers the banking and shopping facilities of a small town. The town, whose name is a corruption of the name 'Austin's', is of historical importance for it was at the Mermaid Tavern that the Articles of Agreement were signed in 1652. The 'Articles' were the terms of surrender that were negotiated between Willoughby's defeated Royalists and Cromwell's forces. The terms were in fact generous and guaranteed the Barbados Assembly a considerable degree of autonomy.

Fishing is still the main activity at Oistins and in recent years its fleet and port facilities have been upgraded. The importance of traditional fishing skills can be appreciated at the annual **Fish Festival** in April when local fishermen and women demonstrate their abilities in fishing, fish-boning and boat racing.

White egrets

Continuing along Highway 7 towards Bridgetown we soon enter the lively south coast resort area which stretches from Maxwell to Hastings. Here you will find a vast assortment of accommodation, residential property, restaurants and shopping plazas. What the visitor can easily miss, however, is a small oasis of nature set in the heart of this development — **Graeme Hall Swamp,** located at Worthing, just behind the big supermarket. Graeme Hall is a mangrove swamp that has become a bird sanctuary. If you visit the swamp towards sunset in winter you will be able to see the flocks of white egret roosting in the mangrove trees. If you are lucky and patient you may even see the red seal coot, a rare species that only nests at Graeme Hall.

And with a visit to Graeme Hall Swamp we round up our set of Barbadian itineraries — have a good trip!

Barbados is rich in parks and gardens. The Flower Forest, high up in the Scotland area is one of the best.

Bibliography

W. Alleyne, *Historic Houses of Barbados,* Barbados National Trust.

M.J. Bourne, G.W. Lennox, S.A. Seddon, *Fruits and Vegetables of the Caribbean,* Macmillan Caribbean, 1988.

E.P. Clark, *West Indian Cookery,* Nelson Caribbean, Revised Edition, 1976.

G. Dann, *Quality of Life in Barbados,* Macmillan Caribbean, 1984.

L. Honychurch, *The Dominica Story,* The Dominica Institute, 1984.

F.A. Hoyos, *Barbados, A History from the Amerindians to Independence,* Macmillan Caribbean, 1978.

F.A. Hoyos, *Barbados, Our Island Home,* Macmillan Caribbean, Third Edition 1979.

F.A. Hoyos, *Barbados, The Visitor's Guide,* Macmillan Caribbean, Second Edition 1988.

G. Lamming, *In the Castle of My Skin,* Longman, 1986.

G.W. Lennox, S.A. Seddon, *Flowers of the Caribbean,* Macmillan Caribbean, 1978.

V.S. Naipaul, *The Overcrowded Baracoon,* Penguin, 1976.

V.S. Naipaul, The Middle Passage, Penguin, 1969.

J.H. Parry, P. Sherlock, A. Maingot, *A Short History of the West Indies,* Macmillan Caribbean, Fourth Edition 1987.

S.A. Seddon, G.W. Lennox, *Trees of the Caribbean,* Macmillan Caribbean, 1980.

R. Wilder (editor), *Barbados,* Apa, 1986.

Appendix B
Wind Force: the Beaufort Scale*

B'fort No:	Wind Descrip.	Effect on land	Effect on sea	Wind Speed			Wave height (m)†
				knots	mph	kph	
0	Calm	Smoke rises vertically	Sea like a mirror	less than 1		-	-
1	Light air	Direction shown by smoke but not by wind vane	Ripples with the appearance of scales; no foam crests	1-3	1-3	1-2	-
2	Light breeze	Wind felt on face; leaves rustle; wind vanes move	Small wavelets; crests do not break	4-6	4-7	6-11	0.15-0.30
3	Gentle breeze	Leaves and twigs in motion wind extends light flag	Large wavelets; crests begin to break; scattered white horses	7-10	8-12	13-19	0.60-1.00
4	Moderate breeze	Small branches move; dust and loose paper raised	Small waves, becoming longer; fairly frequent white horses	11-16	13-18	21-29	1.00-1.50
5	Fresh breeze	Small trees in leaf begin to sway	Moderate waves; many white horses; chance of some spray	17-21	19-24	30-38	1.80-2.50
6	Strong breeze	Large branches in motion; telegraph wires whistle	Large waves begin to form; white crests extensive; some spray	22-27	25-31	40-50	3.00-4.00

7	Near gale	Whole trees in motion; difficult to walk against wind	Sea heaps up; white foam from breaking waves begins to be blown in streaks	28-33	32-38	51-61	4.00-6.00
8	Gale	Twigs break off trees; progress impeded	Moderately high waves; foam blown in well-marked streaks	34-40	39-46	63-74	5.50-7.50
9	Strong gale	Chimney pots and slates blown off	High waves; dense streaks of foam; wave crests begin to roll over; heavy spray	41-47	47-54	75-86	7.00-9.75
10	Storm	Trees uprooted; considerable structural damage	Very high waves, overhanging crests; dense white foam streaks; sea takes on white appearance; visibility affected	48-56	56-63	88-100	9.00-12.50
11	Violent storm	Widespread damage, seldom experienced in England	Exceptionally high waves; dense patches of foam; wave crests blown into froth; visibility affected	57-65	64-75	101-110	11.30-16.00
12	Hurricane	Winds of this force encountered only in Tropics	Air filled with foam & spray; visibility seriously affected	65+	75+	120+	13.70+

* Introduced in 1805 by Sir Francis Beaufort (1774-1857) hydrographer to the Navy

† First figure indicates average height of waves; second figure indicates maximum height.

APPENDIX C: USEFUL CONVERSION TABLES

Distance/Height

feet	ft or m	metres
3.281	1	0.305
6.562	2	0.610
9.843	3	0.914
13.123	4	1.219
16.404	5	1.524
19.685	6	8.829
22.966	7	2.134
26.247	8	2.438
29.528	9	2.743
32.808	10	3.048
65.617	20	8.096
82.081	25	7.620
164.05	50	15.25
328.1	100	30.5
3281.	1000	305.

Weight

pounds	kg or lb	kilograms
2.205	1	0.454
4.409	2	0.907
8.819	4	1.814
13.228	6	2.722
17.637	8	3.629
22.046	10	4.536
44.093	20	9.072
55.116	25	11.340
110.231	50	22.680
220.462	100	45.359

Distance

miles	**km or mls**	kilometres
0.621	1	1.609
1.243	2	3.219
1.864	3	4.828
2.486	4	6.437
3.107	5	8.047
3.728	6	9.656
4.350	7	11.265
4.971	8	12.875
5.592	9	14.484
6.214	10	16.093
12.428	20	32.186
15.534	25	40.234
31.069	50	80.467
62.13	100	160.93
621.3	1000	1609.3

Dress sizes

Size	bust/hip inches	bust/hip centimetres
8	30/32	76/81
10	32/34	81/86
12	34/36	86/91
14	36/38	91/97
16	38/40	97/102
18	40/42	102/107
20	42/44	107/112
22	44/46	112/117
24	46/48	117/122

Tyre pressure

lb per sq in	kg per sq cm
14	0.984
16	1.125
18	1.266
20	1.406
22	1.547
24	1.687
26	1.828
28	1.969
30	2.109
40	2.812

Temperature

centigrade	fahrenheit
0	32
5	41
10	50
20	68
30	86
40	104
50	122
60	140
70	158
80	176
90	194
100	212

Oven temperatures

Electric	Gas mark	Centigrade
225	¼	110
250	½	130
275	1	140
300	2	150
325	3	170
350	4	180
375	5	190
400	6	200
425	7	220
450	8	230

Your weight in kilos

stones

kilograms

Liquids

gallons	**gal or l**	litres
0.220	1	4.546
0.440	2	9.092
0.880	4	18.184
1.320	6	27.276
1.760	8	36.368
2.200	10	45.460
4.400	20	90.919
5.500	25	113.649
10.999	50	227.298
21.998	100	454.596

Some handy equivalents for self caterers

1 oz	25 g	1 fluid ounce	25 ml
4 oz	125 g	¼ pt. (1 gill)	142 ml
8 oz	250 g	½ pt.	284 ml
1 lb	500 g	¾ pt.	426 ml
2.2 lb	1 kilo	1 pt.	568 ml
		1¾ pints	1 litre

Some Carribean recipes

In this section I have included a few Carribean recipes that may interest those who are self-catering in Barbados, or later to prepare at home as tasty reminders of your holiday. The Avocado Pear Soufflé and the Coconut Pie recipes should present no difficulties as far as the ingredients are concerned.

Callaloo Soup

Callaloo Soup is one of the West Indian favourites and is common on most islands. Callaloo are the leaves of dasheen or eddoes. Try using spinach as an alternative.

    12 dasheen or eddo leaves
    a ham bone
    8 or 9 ochroes depending on size
    2 or 3 crabs depending on size
    1 tablespoon of butter
    500ml of water
    1 clove of garlic
    Seasoning to taste

Remove the leaves from the stalks, wash and then roll them. Scald the crabs and clean them well. Wash and cut up the ochroes and the seasonings (including the clove of garlic). Put these ingredients and the ham bone in a saucepan and pour on 500ml of boiling water. Leave to simmer for about 30—45 minutes until everything is soft. Stir well and add butter.

Avocado Pear Soufflé

1 medium sized avocado
2 medium sized eggs
100ml of milk
25g of butter
25g of flour
½ teasp of salt
½ teasp of white pepper

Peel the avocado then grate it. Make a thick white sauce by melting the butter and stirring in first the flour and then the milk. Leave to cool. Separate the eggs, add the yokes to the cooled white sauce and beat well. Whisk the egg whites until they are stiff and then fold into the mixture together with the grated avocado. Add salt and white pepper to taste. Pour the mixture into a well greased pie dish ensuring that you have left enough room for it to rise. Bake for about 30 minutes, the first 15 minutes at 200°C and the remainder of the time at 300°C. The soufflé should be golden brown in colour. Serve immediately.

Creole Fish

Serves 6

900g of cod/kingfish fillet
1 large onion (chopped)
2 cloves of garlic (crushed)
2 spring onions (chopped)
2 limes
500g peeled and sliced tomatoes
25g tomato paste
120ml dry white wine
50g flour
60ml oil

Skin and cut fish into chunks and then marinate in lime juice for 20 minutes. Fry the onion and garlic in half the oil until tender, then add the tomatoes and tomato paste. Stir in and simmer for five minutes. Add the white wine and bring to the boil. Season to taste. Strain the marinated fish and dry with paper. Coat the fish with flour and fry gently in remaining oil until golden brown, but not too well cooked. Put fish in a casserole dish and pour sauce over it. Cover and bake in an oven at 200°C for about 10 minutes. Serve with rice, plantain, dasheen or boiled potatoes.

Coconut Pie

6 Generous Portions
>300g of short crust pastry
>3 eggs
>150g of sugar
>1 cup of grated coconut
>1 cup of milk
>salt

Make the pastry, roll and line a greased pie dish. Prick the bottom with a fork and leave in a refrigerator for about 1 hour. Beat the eggs and add the sugar and a pinch of salt. Boil the milk and stir into the mixture along with the coconut. Pour the mixture onto the pastry and bake at once in a fairly hot oven (200°C). Reduce the heat after about 10 minutes to prevent curdling and bake for a further 30 minutes or until the pastry is golden brown and the filling set.

Papaya Nectar

>1 large papaya (about 2kg)
>1 cup milk
>Juice of 4 limes
>1 teaspoon of grated lime/lemon rind
>100g of sugar
>½ teaspoon of vanilla essence
>1 cup of finely crushed ice

Peel the papaya, cut in half lengthwise and scoop out the seeds, then chop into small chunks. Place all the ingredients in a blender and blend at high speed for about 30 seconds until the mixture is smooth and thick. Serve immediately and garnish with slices of lime.

Tropical Fruit Drink

1 banana
1 ripe mango (skin and stone removed)
1 carrot
500ml of milk
1 egg
Brown sugar to taste
1 teaspoon of lime juice
Vanilla essence and nutmeg to taste
Crushed ice

Place ingredients in blender and blend at high speed until liquified.
Add crushed ice and blend for about another 30 seconds

accommodation 21-9
agriculture 68-9
air services 15-17, 64
 inter-island 36
airlines 15, 37
Andromeda Gardens 128
Animal Flower Cave 116-17
Arawaks 71-2

Bagatelle Great House 124
banana boats 17
banks 37-8
Barbados Board of Tourism 11
Barbados Cherry Tree Orchard
 126
Barbados High Commission 11
Barbados Museum 102
Barbados Turf Club 54
Barbados Wildlife Reserve 62,
 114-15
Barclays Park 127
Barrancoids 71
Bath 136, 139
Bathsheba 128
Bellairs Research Institute 108
Belleplaine 126-7
Belleville 103
bicycle hire 33
birdlife 64
books 38
Boscobelle 116
Bridgetown 95-101
Brighton Beach 106
British High Commission 39
budgeting 12-13
Bulkley Sugar Factory 131
buses 34

calypso 56, 58, 93
Canadian High Commission 39
car hire 32
Careenage 96
Caribs 72-3
Cattlewash 127
Chalky Mount, potteries 126
charter flights 16
Cherry Tree Hill 115
Cherry tree orchard 126

Christ Church 143
 accommodation 22, 26-7, 28
 restaurants 49
churches and cathedral
 All Saints Church 111
 St Andrew's 127
 St George's 130
 St James 107
 St John's 136
 St Lucy's 117
 St Mary's 101
 St Michael's Anglican
  Cathedral 97
 St Peter's 109
 St Thomas 124
cinemas 57
Clifton Hall 136
climate 62
 wind force chart 146-7
clothing 14
coach tours 34
Codrington College 139
communications 64-5
conversion tables 148-51
Cotton Tower 136
Cove Bay 116
Crane Beach 142
cricket 52
cruise ships 18
cruises, coastal 35
Culpepper Island 140
currency 12
customs and duty free 19, 59-60

Deep Water Harbour 64
dinner shows 55-6
discos 57
Drax Hall 134
drinks 47
driving 31-2
driving licences 38
duty free goods 19, 59-60

early settlers 73-6
east coast 127-8
 accommodation 27, 28
 restaurants 49-50
economy 65-9

education 90-1
electricity 38
embassies 39
entertainment 55-8
Erdiston 103
excursions 34-6

Farley Hill National Park 111,
  114
festivals 57-8
fishing 53, 69
flora and fauna 63-4
Flower Forest 124
Folkestone Beach 108
Folkestone Underwater Park 108
food 43-7
 recipes 152-5
Fort Charles 103
Francia 130
fruit 44-7

gardens 63
Garrison Savannah 102
geography 61-2
Gold Coast 21-2
golf 53
government and politics 87-90
Government House 103
Graeme Hill Swamp 64, 143
Grantley Adams International
 Airport 15, 64
Gun Hill 129

Hackleton's Cliff 135
Haggatt's Agricultural Station
 126
handicrafts 60, 100, 101, 126
Harrison's Cave 122
health hazards 40
health precautions 13-14
Heron Bay 108
hiking 54
historical background 71-84
Holetown 106-7
horse races 54
hotels 21-7

houses
  Bagatelle Great House 124
  Drax Hall 134
  Erdiston 103
  Francia 130
  Government House 103
  Illaro Court 103
  Porters House 108
  Sam Lord's Castle 142
  St Nicholas Abbey 115
  Sunbury 140
  Villa Nova 135

Ilaro Court 103
immigration 16, 18-19
information offices 11, 42

jazz 57

Lamming, George 83, 126
Littlegood 117
Lodge School 139

Malvern 135
manicheel trees 40
manufacturing 68
maps
  Barbados 11
  Barbados and Windward Isles 8
  Bridgetown 98-9
  centre and east 120-1
  south 132-3
  St Peter and St Lucy 112-13
  west coast and St Michael 104
markets
  Bridgetown 101
Martin's Bay 136
Maycock's Bay 117
medical facilities 39
Mile and a Quarter 111
Moravian chapel 119
Morgan Lewis Windmill 115
mosquitoes 40
Mount Gay 118
museums
  Barbados Museum 102

museums (cont)
Folkestone 108
Portvale Sugar Machinery
Museum 124
Sunbury 140
music 92-3

Needham's Point 103
Newcastle 136
newspapers 38
night life 55-7
Bridgetown 101
North Point 116

Oistins 143
Oughterson Wildlife Park 140

Paleologus, Ferdinando, tomb
136
passports 18
Pelican Village 101
Pico Teneriffe 116
Pie Corner 116
Porters House 108
Portvale Sugar Machinery
Museum 124
postal services 40
population 85-6
public holidays 41
pubs 57

Queens's Park (Bridgetown) 100

radio 41
Ragged Point 139-40
Rastafarianism 87
recipes, Caribbean 152-5
'Red legs' 136-8
religions 86-7
restaurants 47-50
River Bay 116
roads 31, 65
rum distillery 118

Saddleback 125
sailing 52
Sam Lord's Castle 142
sandflies 40

Sandy Lane Hotel 106
Savannah Club 102
scooter hire 33
scuba and skin diving 51-2
sea travel 17-18, 64
sea urchins 40
self-catering accommodation
27-8, 50
Sharon Moravian Chapel 119
shopping 59-60, 100
Six Men's Bay 117
slavery 77-80
snorkelling 51
social services 92
south-east coast
accommodation 27
restaurants 49
south-west coast
accommodation 22, 26-7, 28
restaurants 48-9
souvenirs 60
Speightstown 109
sports 51-4
Spring Garden Highway 105-6
St Andrew 126-7
St Anne's Fort 103
St George 129-34
St James 106-8
accommodation 21, 24-5, 28
restaurants 48
St John 135-9
St Joseph 124-6
accommodation 27, 28
restaurants 50
St Lucy 116-18
St Michael (incl. Bridgetown)
95-104
accommodation 25
restaurants 48-9
St Michael's Anglican
Cathedral 97
St Nicholas Abbey 115
St Peter 108-16
accommodation 21-2, 24-5, 28
restaurants 48
St Philip 139-42
accommodation 27
restaurants 49

St Thomas 119-24
 restaurants 48
Stavronikita 108
steel bands 56, 93
submarine excursion 35-6
sugar 77
sunburn 40
Sunbury 140
surfing 52
swimming 40, 51

taxis 33
telephones 41
television 41
tennis 54
Tent Bay 128
theatres 57, 93
tipping 41
tourism 66-7
tourist information 11, 42
tourist season 11
travel documents 18
tropical fruit 44-7
Turner Hall Woods 126

US Embassy 39

vaccinations 13
villas 29
Villa Nova 135

walking 54
water 42
water sports 51-2
Welchman Hall Gully 122
west coast 105-9
 accommodation 21-2, 24-5, 28
 restaurants 48
wildlife and wildlife parks 63-4
wind force chart 146-7
windsurfing 52